With Uplifted Head

With Uplifted Head

Preaching Hope

AL MACHIELA

with

DANIEL T. LIOY

Wipf & Stock
PUBLISHERS
Eugene, Oregon

WITH UPLIFTED HEAD
Preaching Hope

ISBN 13: 978-1-4982-5001-6

To my wife,
Mary Joy,
Who, from childhood,
Looked upward to her Eternal Father

"I will look on you with favor and make you
fruitful and increase your numbers,
and I will keep my covenant with you.
You will still be eating last year's harvest
when you will have to move it out to make room
for the new.
I will put my dwelling place among you, and I will
not abhor you.
I will walk among you and be your God,
and you will be my people.
I am the Lord your God,
who brought you out of Egypt so that you would
no longer be slaves to the Egyptians;
I broke the bars of your yoke and enabled you to
walk
with heads held high."
—Leviticus 26:9–13

"So far I haven't come across one scrap of wisdom
in anything you've said.
My life's about over.
All my plans are smashed,
all my hopes are snuffed out—
My hope that night would turn into day,
My hope that dawn was about to break.
If all I have to look forward to is a home in the
graveyard,
If my only hope for comfort is a well-built coffin,
If a family reunion means going six feet under, and
the only family that shows up is worms,
Do you call that hope?
Who on earth could find any hope in that?
No.
If hope and I are to be buried together,
I suppose you'll all come to the double funeral!"
—Job 17:10–16
The Message

Contents

Foreword

Is your congregation glum, dour, or discouraged, perhaps even in despair? Then, pastor, here is the book for you. *With Uplifted Head: Preaching Hope* is a book that, while exalting Christ and giving insight into biblical teaching about hope, shows how to preach in a way that will foster hope among members of your congregation.

This book offers no mere panacea. By carefully examining the enormous amount of material in God's Word regarding hope and noting how modern preaching woefully fails to incorporate this scriptural perspective, Dr. Machiela establishes a solid, biblical case for preaching hope.

But neither is the book theology without soul. Here is a volume that instructs and challenges in an easygoing and sparkling manner.

And furthermore in this book there is plenty of how-to. From it you will learn both how to preach hope directly and indirectly.

In fulfilling the requirements for the Doctor of Ministry program in preaching at Westminster Theological Seminary in California, of which the preparation of this book was a part, Dr. Machiela found that God blessed his efforts in his own congregation and in the churches of other pastors to whom he taught these principles.

Pastor, are you looking for a way to lift your preaching out of the doldrums? Yes? Then, with uplifted head, preach the hope discussed in this book.

Dr. Jay E. Adams
Institute for Nouthetic Studies,
Greenville, South Carolina
Former Director, Doctor of Ministry Program
Westminster Theological Seminary
Escondido, California

Introduction

GOD'S HOPE strengthens the discouraged like no other source of hope in the world. It is powerful, certain, living, and available. It is the only hope tied to eternity in Christ. God's hope—the kind of hope described in this book—encouraged a thoughtful Christian woman, who was distressed by the sudden deaths of her mother and brother, to look up, take heart, and move ahead in her new life with Christ. God's hope was the resource of encouragement that enabled the thirty-one year old typist of the first draft of this book (who experienced a recurrence of Hodgkin's Disease and underwent eight months of chemotherapy while working on the text) to cope with her situation and lean forward in service for the Lord.

Do you have this kind of God-centered hope? Do your friends? And do the people with whom you share your faith? Or do you pass your days with a lump in your throat and a heavy heart? You and your church family need not become mired in despair. Because the Lord is the "God of hope" (Romans 15:13), He is able to "fill you with all joy and peace as you trust in Him, so that you may overflow with hope by the power of the Holy Spirit."

Every believer encounters challenges, frustrations, and opposition. These normal, patience testing aspects of maturing in Christ are like foothills that sometimes block a mountain hiker's view of distant snow-capped peaks. Because Christians know the peaks are there, even though hidden from view, they can push onward and upward.

What is the highest peak of biblical hope? It is the return of Jesus and eternal life in His presence! That hope should lighten every step and quicken the heart of every believer. To possess biblical hope, we must carefully study God's Word and develop a practical understanding of how our future in Christ relates to our daily lives. Yet, that connection is often blurred. This book will help you think through that important relationship.

Pastors, people continually look to you for hope. If you or members of your church say, "Why are you downcast, O my soul?" (Psalm 42:5), you needn't despair or burn out. Biblical hope provides the solution.

Words of Gratitude

BOOKS, LIKE good sermons, take years to write. They are a composite of learning, experience, and reflection. I thank God for men, women, and children who, in many ways, places, and circumstances taught and showed me how to stretch forward to take hold of the things above.

When I think of those I want to thank for having helped shape my perspective of hope I immediately turn to the Christian Reformed Church in North America, the church in which I was raised. Sitting in her pews, rubbing shoulders with her members, and studying in her schools and seminary, I became keenly aware of the need to balance the "already" of godly life today with the "not yet" of future glory.

Though the CRCNA provided the theological foundation from which I learned to view life and the world, my ideas regarding the hope of the gospel were not condensed into a cohesive unit of thought until I began to focus on this subject in my Doctor of Ministry studies at Westminster Seminary in California. So, it is with sincere gratitude that I thank Dr. Jay Adams (D.Min. Program Director) and Dr. Derke Bergsma (my faculty advisor) for their advice and guidance.

One of the first individuals who helped me sense the heavenward tug of hope is my mother. Mom shocked wheat with a song, washed dishes with a song, and raised five boys with a song! Oh, she cried too, but her sobs, as well as her songs, were always aimed heavenward. Thanks, Mom! I've been watching!

Another person, who deserves much credit for helping me write the first draft of this book, is Nancy VanDyken. Nancy challenged unsubstantiated ideas, exposed faulty logic, and rethreaded tangled sentences. She did so while fighting and recovering from Hodgkin's! For Nancy hope was not theory.

After burying the manuscript of this book in my desk for 20 years, Dr. Dan Lioy encouraged me to resurrect and update it. Without Dan and his wife, Marcia, who retyped the entire manuscript, *Uplifted Head,* would still be entombed in my bottom desk drawer.

Finally, I want to thank my family—my wife, Mary, and my four children, Heather, Melody, Nathan, and Joel. They trouped with me through thirty-eight years of ministry, six in Taiwan, 30 in the U.S. and one in the Philippines. Without kids, and puppies, and baseballs, and piano lessons, it would be easy to become so heavenly minded that I would be of no earthly use. My family kept me grounded and real while I tried to point people to the Kingdom that is not of this world.

Certainly, among all those who helped keep my head uplifted and on target, Mary deserves the greatest credit. She listened with discerning ears, discussed and contributed valuable insights she gained through her extensive reading, and she encouraged me as my patient, persistent partner. Thank you, especially, for helping to bring this project to completion by editing and reformatting the manuscript.

CHAPTER ONE

Taking Aim at Despair

HER SHOULDERS slumped as she waited to talk with me after church. Deep worry lines tugged her face into a furled, forlorn expression of grief. A three-year-old swung from her coat sleeve like a pint-sized Tarzan, whining so loudly that I could hardly hear the "secret" spoken from her despondent lips: "My husband is an alcoholic."

Crushing despair overwhelmed Barb. She was trapped in a meaningless vortex. Life had become dismal, depressing, and seemingly hopeless.

As I listened to Barb's story, I wondered why my sermon hadn't helped. What I had preached was biblical and true. Why hadn't it lifted Barb's spirits? Isn't the gospel supposed to alleviate real-life, household discouragement? I knew that it could; yet my message had somehow failed to convey hope.

How hopeful is your preaching? Does the one-third[1] of your congregation that comes to church in discouragement leave with uplifted head? To be sure, sermons are not ecclesiastical pep pills dispensed to make worshipers feel buoyant and cheerful. But they should inject believers with

---

1. Author's estimate, based on interviews with Christian counselors, survey results of eight congregations, and data collected from more than 75 pastors. On the average, it seems, at least one-third of a gathered congregation on any Sunday comes to worship in varying degrees of discouragement, depression, or despair.

purpose—a purpose that propels them forward in life and assures them that they are traveling on the right road.

What is the hope of the gospel, the hope that can dispel the heavy clouds of gloom? Simply stated, it is the anticipation and foretaste of the believer's future in Christ. A sermon lacking this expectation lacks hope, and that's exactly how I'd failed Barb.

Hopeful believers live today in the light of tomorrow. They know why they are in this world. They know where they are going, and they sense the excitement of being part of the emerging, eternal kingdom of their Lord. Hopeful believers are a people who lean ahead to take hold of that for which God has called them heavenward in Christ Jesus (Philippians 3:12).

To preach hope is to preach the forward look. It is to open the door of an eternal future to those whose horizons are limited to the present, the mundane, and the monotonous. God's hope lifts sullen and discouraged faces heavenward for the rays of tomorrow's glory to brighten them. It strengthens feeble arms and weak knees to make them useful to the King.

As a preacher of the gospel, God has assigned to you the delightful task of bringing hope! Paul proclaimed, "But now he has reconciled you by Christ's physical body through death to present you holy in his sight, without blemish and free from accusation—if you continue in your faith, established and firm, not moved from the hope held out in the gospel. This is the gospel that you heard and that has been proclaimed to every creature under heaven, and of which I, Paul, have become a servant" (Colossians 1:22–23). The apostle also urged his successors to stress hope (Titus 3:7–8).

People need this kind of God-given hope. Without it, they drag their feet and eventually perish. But with such hope, they thrive, grow, and press ahead. In hope, people master tough jobs, learn complicated skills, and form new relationships. But in despair, the same people duck challenges and shun meeting others. Hopelessness restricts vision and saps energy. For Christians, hopefulness is essential. Without it, their witness and service flounders.

Despair—Our Enemy

If biblical hope is the expectation and initial experience of our future in Christ, then despair is a futureless, Christless perspective and existence.

The French existentialist, Jean Paul Sartre, epitomized the philosophy of despair in his novel, *Nausea*. Having eliminated science, experience, rational humanism, and even love as satisfactory bases for truth, Sartre concluded that man is superfluous. For Sartre,

> Existence is ugly, bare, and futile. The world is obscene. Man is a creature who demands a reason for being and yet is confronted only by an inhuman, brute world that offers no explanation either for itself or for man. Man's existence in such a world constitutes the absurd.[2]

Long before Sartre's day, the writer of Ecclesiastes expressed similar thoughts with these words, "'Meaningless! Meaningless!' says the teacher, 'Utterly meaningless! Everything is meaningless'" (Ecclesiastes 1:2).

In these poignant cries of despair, we see the unmasked face of our enemy. Despair arises in lives pointed in no direction at all. It overwhelms those with a vacant, hollow, and blank future. It is the fruit of living without purpose.

Despair appears in many forms. Sometimes it displays itself in the furled brow of the depressed and discouraged.

2. Evans, *Existentialism: The Philosophy of Despair and the Quest for Hope*, 51.

At other times it shows up in the frivolous laughter or banter of the rich. Wherever it appears, it conveys the same message: "Empty, empty! My life is empty, and I'm lost!"

The Victims of Despair

All unbelievers suffer from despair. Some of them speed thoughtlessly through life taking the fastest possible lane their status and finances will allow. These people have no idea where they are going or why they are traveling. Their interest is in the journey itself, rather than in the destination. Many try hard to conceal the futility of their existence with their gadgets and games. Their motto is: "Let's eat, drink, and be merry, for the end will never come!"

Others without Christ give more thought to their futility. For them, life is truly depressing. They hate life, but can't figure out how to avoid it. Their lives are summarized by the words imprinted on a T-shirt: "I continue with my relationships because I don't dare commit suicide!"

Although believers have an eternal future in Christ, the web of despair sometimes entangles them too. Lloyd John Ogilvie, former pastor of the Hollywood Presbyterian Church and U.S. Senate chaplain, remarked that what his radio audience wanted most from the Lord was a sense of hope.[3] Sometimes even God's children lose track of where they are going and forget that God cares for them. Job was utterly discouraged. The psalmists often felt defeated. Imprisoned and threatened, John the Baptist questioned his perspective. Peter wept bitterly in shame and confusion.

The dismay and discouragement so familiar to biblical saints is still common to God's people today. I recall a

3. Dr. Ogilvie's sermon included survey results showing that both explicitly and implicitly, the overwhelming need of his radio audience was for hope (*Where There's Hope, There's Life*, from the series, *Always, There Is Hope*).

young lady who told me how she suffered during a torturous period of depression. She had no doubt, she said, about her salvation or heaven. In exhaustion and weakness, though, she failed to experience the nearness of God. She felt abandoned and alone. On another occasion, a pastoral colleague confided that he spent three months in bed, too depressed to get up and answer his door. Another time, I ministered to a strapping young farmer, who through a tragic accident lost the use of his arms and legs. He became a quadriplegic. In an instant, life as he had known it was over. Would he ever be able to care for himself, sit, stand, work, or go fishing? He sank into despair.

None of these Christians questioned their eternal destiny, but they lacked the confidence needed to face the immediate future. The fountain of despair was within them. Some needed rest, medicine, and healing. As Vance Havner puts it, sometimes we need to come apart and rest, or "we may just—come apart!"[4] Others needed to handle trouble differently, for their despair was spiritual. But all needed hope.

Ministers of the gospel should not be surprised when believers become discouraged. Many pastors themselves wrestle with despair. In his book, *Walking With the Giants*, Warren Wiersbe comments, "It seems that depression and discouragement are occupational hazards, if not occupational diseases, of the ministry."[5] He quotes, among others, Charles H. Spurgeon, who lamented, "I am the subject of depressions so fearful that I hope none of you ever get to such extremes of wretchedness as I go to."

4. Dr. Vance Havner is known as one of the most quoted preachers of the twentieth century. See his website, http://www. vancehavnersermons.com/, for further information on the resources available through his ministry.

5. Wiersbe, *Walking With the Giants*, 263.

Of all persons, you as a pastor must know God's remedy for discouragement. People in your pews are looking to you for help. Can you respond? Are you able to escape the pit of despair yourself?

How to Help the Despairing

To be an effective encourager of the despairing, you must first ask what kind of help is needed. Do they have their future secured in Christ? If not, you must teach them the victory of the cross and the hope of the resurrection. Without these, lasting relief is impossible.

Because you do not know if everyone who comes to a corporate worship service is a believer, the power of the cross and the certainty of eternal life in Christ should be included in some way in every sermon. If you do not base your preaching of hope upon these essential truths, your sermons will lack the foundation upon which all biblical hope rests.

Laying the groundwork is a necessary condition for instilling genuine hope. Alone, however, it remains insufficient. Hope-filled preaching regarding all aspects of Christian living must follow. D. W. Cleverly Ford's remarks are apt:

> [Hopeful preaching] cannot stop at the proclamation of the Christ-event and sins forgiven. It must reflect hopefulness in all that it does. Such preaching will stand out in sharp contrast to the world in which it operates. With the erosion of Christian faith in the countries of the West in the latter half of the twentieth century, there has crept over mankind a feeling of hopelessness.[6]

---

6. Ford, *The Ministry of the Word*, 175.

Disheartened saints need to refocus. You must teach them to see Christ in regal glory governing all things for the sake of His church. When they do, they will realize that service rendered in this world on His behalf counts (I Corinthians 15:58)! Further, you must regularly remind them that Jesus is coming soon to judge all people and to make all things new. There is no time to waste and no time to spare.

But even more is necessary. Downcast believers must be assured that the Messiah who reigns and the God who rules is not distant or uncaring; rather, He is present and faithful in love. In fact, His mercy and grace are new every morning!

Barb, the despairing young wife I mentioned earlier, recovered from her sense of hopelessness by internalizing Lamentations 3:19–24, and applying its message in her life: "I remember my affliction and my wandering, the bitterness and the gall. I well remember them, and my soul is downcast within me. Yet this I call to mind and therefore I have hope: Because of the LORD's great love we are not consumed, for his compassions never fail. They are new every morning; great is your faithfulness. I say to myself, 'The LORD is my portion; therefore, I will wait for him.'"

The gospel is a message of hope. It looks ahead to our future in Christ and helps us begin to take hold of it. Many preachers major on faith and love, but neglect hope. Therefore, those who come to worship in despair often leave as they came. Or worse, longing for hope, they do not receive it. The preacher failed them and they leave disappointed again. They reason, "Surely God can give me hope," but when no hopeful note is sounded from the pulpit, they wonder.

Our world today is crying for hope. In 1985, French scholar and teacher Jacques Ellul commented that "we are in a crisis situation and we're going to have an increasing number of people who live in anguish and despair, fearing tomorrow."[7] Two decades later it is apparent that his prediction has come true! In writing the following, Cornelius Plantinga Jr., the president of Calvin Theological Seminary, contrasts the world today with "the way things are supposed to be":

> Sad to say, we now see around us only small approximations of this great state of affairs. In fact, we have a world troubled enough that human hope—sometimes wistful, sometimes desperate—will be a growth industry for some time to come. Everyone knows there is something about human life that is out of line or out of whack. We can be happy at times, but not totally fulfilled. Even when we have happiness, we fear we'll lose it. Worse, every day brings us fresh news of old evils—or nature ravaged, of God blasphemed, of people cheated, battered, terrorized. Every day brings us news of people whose misery is almost impossible to fathom.[8]

Everywhere we turn we witness the grinding effect of grief and pain. The members of your congregation need to learn how to cope in such an environment and see beyond it. God's Word provides you, as their pastor, with the words of encouragement that your people need. Feed them and watch their heads lift heavenward!

7. As quoted in Russell H. Heddendorf, "Christians in the World, but not of the World," *Presbyterian Journal*, January 1 and 8, 1986, p. 8.

8. Plantinga Jr., *Engaging God's World: A Reformed Vision of Faith, Learning, and Living*, 15.

CHAPTER TWO

Focus of Biblical Hope

HOPEFUL PEOPLE are goal oriented. They know where they are going and how they will get there. Adversity cannot deter them. Preaching that engenders hope shows people the way ahead. It offers a map for life and beckons people onward. Does your preaching say, "Come, let's serve the Lord as we wait to enter His presence"?

A Certain Hope

The goal of the Christian life is not imaginary. It is real, tangible, and certain. Therefore, *hope* might seem to be an inappropriate word to describe our anticipation of attainment. For example, you would hardly expect a woman in her eighth month of pregnancy to say longingly, "I hope I will have a baby." With normal development, it is inevitable. But if she uses the term *hope* as it is used in the Bible, even in the final days of pregnancy she would say that she hopes to give birth. According to biblical usage, we hope for what is absolute and sure because we wait for that which God has promised (Romans 8:18–25).

Since common parlance and biblical usage of the term *hope* diverge, it is necessary for you, as a preacher, to make clear that hope in the scriptural sense is the opposite of what we often mean when we wistfully say, "I surely hope so."

Biblical hope is not "a wish strongly tinged with doubt,"[1] as when a lazy student crosses his or her fingers "hoping" to pass the exam, or when an ill-qualified applicant holds his or her breath "hoping" to be hired. It is not hanging onto a thread or wishing the improbable. Nor is it a "pipe dream, reverie, mirage, castle in the air, or utopia"[2] as *Roget's Thesaurus* suggests. Biblical hope is the anticipation or expectation of an irrevocably certain future in Christ that has already begun to unfold.

Unlike groundless optimism, biblical hope is absolutely certain. Though optimists believe what they hope for is possible and even likely, their dreams may remain unfulfilled. Even rainbow-optimism does not prevent the unexpected sale of profitable corporations that promise bright futures to their aspiring executives.

Pollyanna cannot protect the overstrained ligaments upon which the careers of football running backs are carried. Even Pandora's hope—the hope that burns eternal in the human heart and always believes that there is a way—cannot stabilize the shifting sands of the future. Only Christian hope, anchored like steel shafts driven into the solid rock of God's person and His Word, can accomplish that!

I am not demeaning optimism. But optimism unrelated to Christ is a flimsy substitute for biblical hope. Putting the most favorable construction upon actions and happenings, and sanguinely anticipating the best possible outcome of events and circumstances, is far removed from organizing all of life around a certain and glorious future in Christ.

I know someone who is a super-salesperson. When customers enter her store, she pursues them like a mosquito targeting a victim. She intends to "get them" and she is

1. Moule, *The Meaning of Hope, Biblical Series-5*, 4.
2. Lewis, editor, *Roget's Thesaurus in Dictionary Form*, 199.

usually successful. Because she knows how to sell and close a deal, she's almost always optimistic about sales potential and career development. But sadly her optimism has very little to do with her Christian faith or the goal of her life. In contrast, someone who has biblical hope considers how all the spheres of human existence fit together and contribute to the grand purpose of living to the glory of God and entering His magnificent presence.

Hundreds of passages and many metaphors of Scripture teach the certainty of the believer's hope. For instance, Psalm 62 claims God as the source of hope and describes Him as a "rock" of security and salvation: "My soul will never be shaken . . . Find rest, O my soul, in God alone; my hope comes from him" (verses 1, 2, and 5).

Only God is able to serve as the stable ground and fountain of hope, for He alone is the trustworthy object of hope. As "the Hope of Israel" (Jeremiah 14:8–9), He can be counted on to help those in distress (Psalm 27:5–6). By trusting in the Lord, the hearts of the faint become resolute and courageous: "Surely God is my salvation; I will trust and not be afraid. The LORD, the LORD, is my strength and my song; he has become my salvation" (Isaiah 12:2).

In His sovereign grace, God enables His people to wait silently for Him.[3] Patience to wait is not, of course, a natural instinct. It is a quality God must gradually instill. Therefore, it is not surprising that elderly believers are frequently the most hopeful adult members of the church family. By walking far with a hand in God's, they have found Him faithful. One writer makes this pertinent observation:

---

3. All the five major Hebrew terms that are rendered as "hope" (*batah, hasa, yahal, gawa,* and *sabar,* which in the Greek are *elpis* and *elpizo*) express confidence and trust in God's faithful love (Hebrew, *hsd*). Because God does not change and His promises must be fulfilled, we are wise to wait for Him.

> Over and over again in the Old Testament, this refrain is sounded. God alone is the hope of the individual, of the covenant community, and of the whole creation. Therefore, the person who hopes in God manifests this hope by the power to wait silently for Him and by the confidence in an impregnable refuge (cf. Isaiah 12:2; 25:4; 30:15; 32:17; Jeremiah 14:8; 17:13; Deuteronomy 32: 1–43; 33:26–29). Hope is a word, then, that does not point to what a man has in himself, or to what God does by Himself; rather, it signifies what God by His faithful work instills in man and what man by his patient trust attributes to God.[4]

Since the covenant-making and covenant-keeping God of the Old Testament is also the God of the New Testament, the early church vested the same confidence in Him as their spiritual predecessors. Regardless of age or generation, the reason for confidence in God is always the same. It is His reliability proven through fulfillment of past promises and predictions. Dutch theologian Hendrikus Berkhof accurately depicts Israel's approach to the future as the following:

> The continuation, confirmation, extension, and fulfillment of what God has accomplished in the past and present. . . . Faithful Israel had access to the unknown future because it knew about past and present and believed in the faithfulness of its God. We may say that the eschatology of Israel is the confession of God's faithfulness on the screen of the future.[5]

---

4. Minear, *Christian Hope and the Second Coming*, 21.
5. Berkhof, *Well-Founded Hope*, 17.

Depressed, despondent, lonely, and suffering people need to hear that the God of history is reliable. When they do, they'll take heart. Read Psalm 46, for example, to a dying believer and explain that almighty God, the God of Jacob, is his or her fortress. You'll see the confident smile of assurance. Point out how Jesus Christ, crucified, risen, and ascended, satisfies the Old Testament predictions of Moses, Isaiah, and Jeremiah, and that as our faithful God and Savior, Jesus is our hope (I Timothy 1:1). Show these languishing Christians that as God, Jesus, is . . .

> a refuge and a fortress, the source and sustainer of life (I Corinthians 10:4; John 6:35; 11:25) . . . a foundation and a cornerstone, the rock on which false hopes are crushed and on which true hope is built (Romans 9:33; I Corinthians 1:23; Mark 12:10; I Peter 2:4–7; Ephesians 2:20–22) . . . [He] is the light, the Dayspring which discloses the vanity of darkness and leads men into the perfect day (John 8:12; Revelation 2:28) . . . the first and the last (Revelation 1:17).[6]

People rejoice in a God who is strong and eternally present. Proclaim Him and you will surely bring confidence and joy to your people.

Preachers of hope, who are sure of God and His promises, point often to the record of His mighty acts. God's record is perfect. He has never broken a promise nor met an opposing force He could not move. What He says, He does. When He moves, He creates His own path. He is totally trustworthy and dependable. No person or power in the entire world even remotely compares with Him. Thus, all hopes, except hope in God, are mundane and futile. Psalm 33:16–22 speaks of this hope in striking poetic meter:

6. Minear, *Christian Hope and the Second Coming*, 22.

> No king is saved by the size of his army; no warrior escapes by his great strength. A horse is a vain hope for deliverance; despite all its great strength it cannot save. But the eyes of the LORD are on those who fear him, on those whose hope is in his unfailing love, to deliver them from death and keep them alive in famine. We wait in hope for the LORD; he is our help and our shield. In him our hearts rejoice, for we trust in his holy name. May your unfailing love rest upon us, O LORD, even as we put our hope in you.

God is trustworthy! With hope in Him, a wife of an alcoholic, a man without employment, and a teenage son of a father who committed suicide, can still hope. In fact, they can even rejoice in the midst of pain, for God is in control and will keep His promises. When life itself seems to be eroding, God and His Word provide hope.

Hope in the Lord is different from all other hopes. It alone has no disappointment factor. After all, God does not fail. If we are disappointed regarding our hope, we are mistaken about the divine promise. God has never neglected one of His promises, and we can be sure that He will not begin to do so now.

Because God is failure-proof and we are failure-prone, we should never fault God for neglecting to keep what we imagined His promises to be. Gardens have weeds and roses have thorns; similarly, God never promised a trouble-free life. Yet, that is what we sometimes believe.

I recall a young entrepreneur who angrily refused to go to church because he lost big money on an apartment house investment. His faithfulness in serving God, he claimed, had not been rewarded by God's protection. The young man, charging God with victimizing the innocent, challenged the Lord to account for His actions. Regrettably, the man had turned the tables on God and, in effect, made himself the "faithful one." After pushing God aside, the offended, self-righteous young man seated himself on the throne of his life.

What a pitiful situation when a person misunderstands God's promises, climbs on His throne, and spits in the face of God! Believers must understand that the Lord uses trials to nourish hope, not destroy it (Romans 5:2–5; James 1:2–4). The young entrepreneur's hope was a false, unbiblical one, centered on self and the here-and-now.

One of God's central promises undergirding true hope is His guarantee that He will carry to completion the good work He begins in His children (Philippians 1:6). What confidence this promise creates, especially when rightly understood and applied. We have been called heavenward in Christ Jesus (Colossians 3:1–4). Our goal is clear and certain! Therefore, we must press on to take hold of that for which we have been taken hold of by God (Philippians 3:12–14). Dr. John MacArthur, pastor of Grace Community Church in Panorama City, California, explains the consistent work of God in believers in this way:

> If He pre-established a love relationship with an individual, He did not only predestinate him to enter in, but predestined him ultimately to be in the image of Christ. . . . We are not predestined to be incomplete, but to be complete. Whom He predestined to be called, He predestined to be glorified. There is no loss. If you are predestined to begin, you are predestined to end. If you are predestined to start, you are predestined to finish. If you are predestined to be in Christ, you are predestined to be like Christ.[7]

7. John MacArthur, Sermon Tape GC 45–41, "The Security of Salvation," Part 2, 1982.

No matter what our circumstances, God wants us to overflow with hope by the Holy Spirit and to be filled with all joy and peace as we trust in Him (Romans 15:13). God's Word and Spirit enable us, as the author of Hebrews says, to permanently anchor our souls behind the curtain in God's heavenly sanctuary, where Jesus entered on our behalf, and moor on the rock of that eternal land (Hebrews 6:16–20).

Hope is stronger than wish. It is a confident desire for what God has promised. In light of this truth, and as a preacher of the Word, lift your head high and proclaim the only message in the world that cannot disappoint! Don't dilute, negotiate, weaken, or conceal God's message, as I did one time as a youngster.

One sultry day at the county fair, my little buddy and I stopped to rest our weary legs in "Noah's Ark" (as it was called). We both knew the Bible story and thought it a little strange that the ark should settle on the thoroughfare of the fairgrounds; but we never guessed it was a trap! It was just that, however, and we were the victims. Even before we had time to set the few trinkets and gadgets of our day's winnings on the floor, who but Mrs. Noah should appear. She was stout, plump, and scary. We were caught and we knew it.

Since I was taught to respect Bible stories and realized that attentiveness would be the quickest way out, I said "yes" to every question that she asked, even the one about whether I wished to receive Christ as my personal Savior. Mentally congratulating myself for my cleverness, I was unprepared for Mrs. Noah's next move.

"Well," she said, "let's go out and tell someone the exciting news of what happened to you!"

I had no choice; all I could do was punctuate my deceptive performance with a blatant lie. So I did. "I'm sorry, ma'am," I said, "but I can't. I'm beginning to feel sick."

Thankfully, Mrs. Noah understood how impossible it is for sick children to be missionaries. But God does not accept the phony excuses of preachers whom He has commissioned to declare His unbreakable promises of hope.

Because you are ordained to preach the Word, you must herald the truth. God has called you to stand on the record of His fulfilled promises and confidently announce hope for the future. Your task is to "declare his glory among the nations, his marvelous deeds among all peoples" (Psalm 96:3). Your congregation will move ahead in hope when they are sure that the Lord, who promises, is faithful.

Hope Points Ahead

True hope always has a future reference. Hope that is already realized is not biblical in nature (Romans 8:24). This is why some of my favorite definitions of hope breathe expectancy. "Hope is 'faith on tiptoe.'"[8] "Christian hope is the construal of our future in terms of God's promises of eternal life and righteousness."[9]

Hope is faith looking forward. Which way does your preaching look? Ahead? If so, how far? My purpose in writing this book is to encourage you to preach with uplifted head in eager expectation of what lies ahead in Christ, and to teach your congregation to embrace the same perspective.

Because of your preaching, your congregants should be able to understand how their hope relates to the hope of God's people throughout history and how they share a common, but more complete, vision of the future with their predecessors. Church members must be able to set their aspirations of hope in the context of the past and future

8. Moule, *The Meaning of Hope*, 11.
9. Roberts, *Spirituality and Human Emotion,* 98.

in such a way that they are equipped to mold the world around them into the shape of the world to come.

For your church to develop this type of balanced, historically sensitive, and hope-filled perspective, your preaching must reflect the biblical sense of *sojourn*. To determine the extent to which this concept is conveyed in pulpits today, I listened to about two hundred of my colleagues' sermons. I found that most of their messages were solidly biblical and dealt with significant aspects of Christian living. A few were "positive thinking" messages. But hardly any pictured believers as a people on the move, traveling from point A to point B, with the glory ahead as a reason or motivating force for today.

If your preaching is to create hopeful anticipation like that of the Old Testament prophets and New Testament apostles, you must be clear about three facts. First, you must know how to distinguish hope from faith. Second, you must be able to identify your place in redemptive history. And third, you must clearly specify the goal toward which you are moving.

Distinguishing Hope from Faith

First of all, how does faith differ from hope? Faith and hope are necessarily interrelated, but not identical. According to Hebrews 11:1, faith "is being sure of what we hope for and certain of what we do not see." Faith is belief or conviction. Hope is longing or eager expectation. Hope grasps what faith believes, but does so with an eye to the future. Faith believes what hope longs for and does so with certainty. Because faith and hope are interdependent, faith is sometimes said to provide the forward impetus that we would normally attribute to hope.

Perhaps it is easiest to distinguish faith from hope by looking at passages in which the faith-hope-love triad is used. Although love is the greatest of this close-knit three-some, hope undergirds its companions.

In Titus 1:1–2, Paul pictured hope as the foundation upon which the walls of faith and knowledge and a roof of godliness were constructed: "Paul, a servant of God and an apostle of Jesus Christ for the faith of God's elect and the knowledge of the truth that leads to godliness—a faith and knowledge resting on the hope of eternal life, which God, who does not lie, promised before the beginning of time."

Hope is the spring rain and warm air that nurtures Christian fruit bearing. It fructifies the believer's life so that attractive fruit germinates and grows to the glory of God. Without living hope, faith and godliness become unproductive and yield only scrawny, shriveled examples of what quality Christian fruit can be.

In Colossians 1:5–6, Paul used another metaphor—that of a fountain—to illustrate how faith, hope, and love relate. Faith and love, he said, "spring from the hope that is stored up for you in heaven." According to I Thessalonians 1:2–3 hope inspires endurance. It keeps you going. Faith produces work. Love prompts labor. But if hope dries up, work and labor also stop flowing.

It's all too easy to find examples of fixed, frozen, boring, and motionless faith. I remember the Christian teenager who wished she could be dead for a while and then come back to life. Though she could recite every doctrine in the catechism, her faith seemed meaningless, as purposeless and unrelated to her real life as her French studies. For her French to come alive, she needed to plan a trip to France! And for her faith to become life changing, she needed to anticipate entering heaven. If she had heard your sermon last week, would her faith zero in on a goal and be drawn to it?

Our Place in Redemptive History

Second, for your preaching to generate authentic biblical hope, you must identify your place in redemptive history. I am not suggesting that you try your hand at date setting. Such efforts are doomed to failure; even Christ said He didn't know the exact time of His return (Matt. 24:36).

But you must know that the redemptive purposes of God are moving ahead on schedule. You must also realize that we are living in the last days (Heb. 1:1–2),[10] that we already have been delivered from the dominion of darkness and transferred to the kingdom of the Son (whom the Father loves; Colossians 1:13), and that we already possess the first fruits of that eternal kingdom (I Corinthians 15:20, 23; James 1:18).[11]

We are nearer to the full revelation of the kingdom of Christ than Old Testament saints were; in fact, the light of God's kingdom shines more brightly for us than it did for them. Living between the "already" of Christ's first coming and the "not-yet" of His return, we have now begun to experience and participate in the initial realities of eternal glory. As we sample the glories ahead, our longing intensifies for the day when the partial will become complete (I Corinthians 13:12).

Reflecting on this contrast, Peter compares what the Old Testament prophets longed to see in the future with what New Testament believers had come to understand and experience.

10. Theologians understand the last day to be the final eschatological time when, at Jesus' return, the wicked are judged and the upright are redeemed. See Gruenler, "Last Day, Days," in *Evangelical Dictionary of Theology*, 670–671.

11. The relationship of hope to the kingdom of God is specifically addressed in chapter five.

> Concerning this salvation, the prophets who spoke of the grace that was to come to you, searched intently and with greatest care, trying to find out the time and circumstances to which the Spirit of Christ in them was pointing when he predicted the sufferings of Christ and the glories that would follow. It was revealed to them that they were not serving themselves but you, when they spoke of those things that have now been told you by those who have preached the gospel to you by the Holy Spirit sent from heaven. Even angels long to look into these things. (I Peter 1:10–12)

Standing in the grace available to us in these last days, we look back to Christ's first coming. As the center of history, He fulfilled the prophetic promise and confirmed forever God's covenant purpose. Since Jesus sealed history with His blood, we confidently and eagerly look forward to its culmination, the return of Christ and the revealing of the sons of God (Romans 8:18–25). If such an orientation permeates your preaching, your ministry will be used of God to help create proper, vibrant, biblical hope.

The Target of Hope

By knowing the God who promises, and by living in the power of His Spirit, you look ahead to the future. But what precisely is the focus of your expectation? In short, it is the return of the Messiah. Consider the following verses:

> For the grace of God that brings salvation has appeared to all men. It teaches us to say "No" to ungodliness and worldly passions, and to live self-controlled, upright and godly lives in this present age, while we wait for the blessed hope—the glorious appearing of our great God

and Savior, Jesus Christ, who gave himself for
us to redeem us from all wickedness and to pu-
rify for himself a people that are his very own,
eager to do what is good. (Titus 2:11–14)

Philippians 3:20–21 also identifies Jesus' coming
as the focal point of our hope: "But our citizenship is in
heaven. And we eagerly await a Savior from there, the Lord
Jesus Christ, who, by the power that enables him to bring
everything under his control, will transform our lowly bodies so that they will be like his glorious body."

These verses are only a few of the passages in Scripture
that pinpoint the focus of hope on the return of Jesus Christ
and the resurrection of the dead. There are many more! For
example, when Paul defended himself before Felix, the
apostle said: "I admit that I worship the God of our fathers,
as a follower of the Way, which they call a sect. I believe
everything that agrees with the Law and that is written in
the Prophets, and I have the same hope in God as these
men, that there will be a resurrection of both the righteous
and the wicked" (Acts 24:14–15).

Before Herod Agrippa II, Paul described himself as being on trial for the Christian hope: "And now it is because of
my hope in what God has promised our fathers that I am on
trial today. This is the promise our twelve tribes are hoping
to see fulfilled as they earnestly serve God day and night.
O king, it is because of this hope that the Jews are accusing
me. Why should any of you consider it incredible that God
raises the dead?" (Acts 26:6–8).

To the Galatians, Paul wrote as follows, "By faith we
eagerly await through the Spirit the righteousness for which
we hope" (Galatians 5:5). The apostle's prayer for believers
in Ephesus was as follows: "[T]hat the eyes of your heart
may be enlightened in order that you may know the hope
to which he has called you, the riches of his glorious inheri-

tance in the saints" (Ephesians 1:18). And as Paul neared death, he rejoiced in the hope of the crown of righteousness that would be awarded on the day when Christ returns:

> I am already being poured out like a drink offering, and the time has come for my departure. I have fought the good fight, I have finished the race, I have kept the faith. Now there is in store for me the crown of righteousness, which the Lord, the righteous Judge, will award me on that day—and not only to me, but also to all who have longed for His appearing. (II Timothy 4:6–8)

Like Paul, Peter identified the resurrection as that which gives birth to hope and makes holiness imperative:

> Praise be to the God and Father of our Lord Jesus Christ! In his great mercy he has given us new birth into a living hope through the resurrection of Jesus Christ from the dead, and into an inheritance that can never perish, spoil, or fade—kept in heaven for you, who through faith are shielded by God's power until the coming of the salvation that is ready to be revealed in the last time. In this you greatly rejoice, though now for a little while you may have had to suffer grief in all kinds of trials. (I Peter 1:3–6)

> You ought to live holy and godly lives as you look forward to the day of God and speed its coming. That day will bring about the destruction of the heavens by fire, and the elements will melt in the heat. But in keeping with his promise we are looking forward to a new heaven and a new earth, the home of righteousness. So then, dear friends, since you are looking

forward to this, make every effort to be found spotless, blameless and at peace with Him. (II Peter 3:11b–14; see also I Peter 1:13)

Why is the return of Jesus and the resurrection of the dead the focal point of hope? It is because these two up-coming events signal the introduction of eternal life into this dying world. Every hope that is not focused on the resurrection is a passing and dying hope; but the hope that is centered on the resurrection is a "living hope" (I Peter 1:3). Here we see that Christian hope is unique. It is distinct from every other form of hope. Christian hope lives, while all other hopes die.

Clustered around the hope of Jesus' second coming are a plethora of blessings: perfect righteousness, perfect communion with God, perfect love among people; perfect transformation, renewal, and flowering of culture; perfect physical well-being, and perfect natural splendor. But the event that triggers the actualization of all these glories is the physical return of our Lord; therefore, His second advent must be the central element in your expectation and proc-lamation of hope.

How to Preach Hope

Let's distill what we have been saying about the focus of hope into a few preaching principles.

1. Hope implies certainty about our future in Christ. Biblical hope is not a "maybe." It is a confident waiting, in holiness, for the full revelation of Christ and His image-reflecting re-creation.

2. Preaching that inspires biblical hope is forward looking. Abraham, David, the Old Testament prophets, the New Testament missionaries, and such

apostles as John, Peter, and Paul, all looked ahead with eyes of hope because of God's faithfulness in the past. You must encourage believers to do the same.

3. All of your preaching must have a hopeful dimension. Living hope is the foundation of growing faith and godliness. Without such hope, doctrinal and ethical teachings are stagnant and incapable of motivating people.

4. Although the accompaniments of Jesus' return, such as the full realization of His kingdom, may legitimately be regarded as the goal of the Christian life, don't forget that His second coming itself is the event for which our eyes turn heavenward. Therefore, preach this truth often.

5. Since Jesus suffered, died, arose, and ascended, and the Holy Spirit already resides in us, the hope that you preach is a living one. It is neither an opiate nor pie-in-the-sky, but real and tangible. It is eternal life in shoes! Indeed, we do not . . .

> enter the door of Christian hope by accepting an inherited doctrine of the Second Coming, but by being transformed into heirs through the death and resurrection of Christ. It is through the manifestation of His dying and rising in our mortal bodies that hope is nourished toward the day of His appearing. Until we live on that level of existence, the shape of our hope will be limited to two alternatives: a spurious otherworldliness that consigns this world permanently to the devil, or a spurious this worldliness that treats the heavenly city as

sheer illusion. The incarnate and suffering Son of God has destroyed both these alternatives for all time.[12]

Thoughtful people ponder what the future holds. You can help them! Advanced technology and science are sure to treat many external ills, but only biblical hope, focused on the resurrection and affirmed by the renewing Holy Spirit, can change us internally and provide life for a future in the presence of the living God.

12. Minear, *Christian Hope and the Second Coming*, 207–208.

CHAPTER THREE

Incomplete Views of Hope (Part One)

WHAT HOPE do you offer to those who are troubled, who seem to have lost their way in life? Is the person who sinks in financial quagmire or who is attacked by volley after volley of character destroying words hearing a consistent and well-rounded message of hope from your pulpit? Expressed differently, are your members being taught how to view their daily struggles in the light of the return of Jesus and His emerging kingdom?

Some preachers offer worshipers an incomplete view of hope. Without deliberately aiming to deceive their hearers, they find the future of Christ and His church a vague inducement for hopeful living. And, in order to be "relevant," they concentrate on success for the here and now. As a result, they seldom discuss the eternal future in Christ with their members. In fact, they rarely speak of "going home" as saints of the past often did, and they do not have a strong sense of participation in the coming kingdom of Christ.

One of the most popular incomplete messages of hope taught from American pulpits today may generally be categorized as "positive thinking."[1] I include under this rubric any form of preaching that deliberately avoids aspects of the

---

1. Voskuil, *Mountains into Goldmines: Robert Schuller and the Gospel of Success,* 55; and Hunt and McMahon, *The Seduction of Christianity: Spiritual Discernment in the Last Days,* 15.

gospel that might offend listeners.[2] "New Age" spirituality is a second weak and unbiblical message of hope. Though it came to prominence two decades ago, it is still prevalent today.[3] Two other inadequate views are dispensational premillennialism and theological liberalism. I will discuss the deficiencies of the first two expressions of hope in this chapter and the shortcomings of the last two in the next chapter.

Unbiblical Positive Thinking

Scripture encourages a God-centered form of positive thinking. Believers are instructed to think about whatever is true, lovely, admirable, excellent, or praiseworthy (Philippians 4:8), and to set their hearts on "things above, where Christ is seated at the right hand of God" (Colossians 3:1). Therefore, to obey the Lord, Christians must become "positive thinkers."

Glum, unhappy, "impossibility thinkers" are influenced by the spirit of Satan. I am sure you are familiar with "negative thinkers." They constantly vote against exciting church program proposals because they are "sure" they won't work. Children at church trouble them because they run and spill juice and cookie crumbs on the floor. Adult church members also irritate them because they are too "lazy" to return supplies and furniture to where they found them. Unlike fellow church workers who wear thin the soles

2. For example, the biblical concepts of sin and repentance.

3. New age spirituality is practiced by some who are in the upper echelons of national government in the U.S. For instance, Ohio Congressman and former 2004 Democratic presidential candidate Dennis Kucinich declares himself to be a "devotee of the New Age movement" (Veith, "Keeping the Faiths," *World Magazine*, 28). Therefore, the speeches he gives are "full of references to cosmic oneness, the interrelatedness of the universe, and mystical spirituality."

of their shoes in service, these grumps wear out their heels by digging in and dragging the church to a standstill. Their attitude is contrary to godly positive thinking.

While Scripture teaches us to be positive, we must be careful that our positive constructions of faith honor the sovereign and gracious character of God. People who perceive faith as a power directed at God, by which He can be forced to accede to their wishes, maintain an unbiblical view of faith. They often set their hope on what *they* want rather than on God's promises for the future. Unbiblical positive thinking neither holds God in high esteem nor prizes the treasures He has in store for those who love Christ's appearing (II Timothy 4:8).

Hope in a Deity Who Can Be Controlled

The God of the Bible is not a puppet. He does not ask, "How high?" when we tell Him to jump. Nor does He make dreams come true just because we attribute them to Him.

Some time ago, a young, ambitious pastor moved his family across the country to start a "great new church." Although he lacked the gifts necessary for effective pastoring and teaching, he was sure God would bless his "vision." Years later, fewer than ten people comprised his congregation. Anger at God seethed within the minister. His earlier "vision" was neither divinely-inspired nor scripturally supported; it was the wishful thinking of a man who tried to manipulate the God who has no strings to pull.

Today, churchmen and secular entrepreneurs alike appear obsessed by "visioneering." Visions may indeed be divinely inspired. But, they also may be merely human constructs of one's own grandiose plans. If your visions of what you feel called to do and accomplish do not reflect the mind, values and life-patterns of the Incarnate Son, their origin is suspect. Even prayer and fasting offer no guarantee that the dreams dancing in your head are of divine origin. If you "pray and fast" to discern God's will, be careful that your food deficient insights are indeed God's and not simply the ideas of a person who is twisting God's arm to get what he wants. Genuine prayer and fasting is waiting upon God for His help.

The Lord is sovereign. He spoke the world into being. He sculptured the course of history and it cannot overflow its predetermined contours. He knows the end from the beginning. Not one of His promises has ever failed, for He is God![4]

Biblical faith is not a positive force. It is a lack of force.[5] It is a giving up on self-reliance, distrust in one's own power, and a casting of one's weak, faltering, stumbling, and sinning self upon the will, promises, and power of almighty God. Such faith rests peacefully in His sovereign arms.

Hope grows when people learn to rest on God's gracious promises and will. Several years ago a young man who had self-righteously pummeled his wife into submission came into my office to confess his sin and ask for guid-

---

4. These truths resonate throughout God's appearance to Job, as recorded in Job 38:1—42:6. In particular, we learn that, because God is absolutely sovereign, He is not obligated to give to those who obey Him what they might desire. Whatever He does or permits to happen is based on His graciousness and righteousness. As the benevolent Lord of the universe, God determines the course of history according to His own hidden plan. God ordains that His children walk in sorrow and pain, sometimes because of sin, sometimes to discipline them, sometimes to strengthen them, and sometimes to reveal His comfort and grace in them. In the end, believers might never know the specific reason for their suffering; nevertheless, they must submit to almighty God and accept by faith that He has a good plan for them.

5. This doesn't mean faith equates with lethargy and lack of energy (see Hebrews 11 and Galatians 5:6). It means we cannot earn our salvation and peace with God by gritting our teeth and trying harder.

ance. The moment he knelt in prayer, acknowledging both his sin and God's forgiving grace, the door of hope swung wide open! For the first time in his life he internalized the truth that sin was the root of his rage, that he could be forgiven, and that Christ could transform his attitude. Relief and confidence immediately flooded the young man's heart. He discovered real hope, the hope that comes from trusting God's sovereign grace.

The deity of growing masses of Americans today is not the great, forgiving, and almighty "I AM WHO I AM" (Exodus 3:14) revealed in Scripture.[6] Instead, they worship a deity who can be sized up, tapped, forced, and controlled. He is a trivialized, man-conceived god who can be pinned down by the person who has figured out his or her "laws for success."

Several discerning Christian leaders have sounded the alarm about the breadth and diversity of this continuing threat to biblical faith. Douglas R. Groothuis, though skeptical of the conspiratorial nature of the New Age movement,[7] sees it as "the thinking and philosophy of the avant-garde middle class which is so strategic in formulating what the American of tomorrow is to be."[8] Groothuis' assessment of the broad appeal of the New Age movement corresponds with statistics found in a March, 2007, internet article regarding New Age Spirituality. It says that, "Recent

6. See Hunt and McMahon, *Seduction,* 11, 57, 91, 151, and 213.

7. The New Age movement is not an organized faction, but an increasingly popular faith perspective that merges science and religion. It also exalts mind power, religious technique, and the possibility of tapping into God via intimate knowledge of His cosmic routine, thus forcing Him to provide what is desired. It appears in many forms and is especially well-received by those whose chief aim in life is to succeed. For further information, see Lardie et al., *Concise Dictionary of the Occult and New Age,* 183–184.

8. Orme, "New Age: Religion of the Avant-Garde Middle Class," 14.

surveys of U.S. adults indicate that many Americans hold at least some new age beliefs:

- 8% believe in astrology as a method of foretelling the future
- 7% believe that crystals are a source of healing or energizing power
- 9% believe that Tarot Cards are a reliable base for life decisions
- About 1 in 4 believe in a non-traditional concept of the nature of God which are often associated with New Age thinking:

    ◊ 11% believe that God is *"a state of higher consciousness that a person may reach"*

    ◊ 8% define God as "*the total realization of personal, human potential"*

    ◊ 3% believe that each person is God.[9]

Commenting on this phenomenon, Hank Hanegraaff of the Christian Research Institute states that adherents of the New Age movement "share common values and a common vision which allow them to cooperate, or network, with one another in order to mold society according to their views of how the world should be." Their pantheistic beliefs have "already made significant inroads into such fields as education, business, and health care, and, to a lesser degree, politics and science."[10]

Central to New Age philosophy is belief in cosmic oneness and the "unity of reality." Reality, according to New

9. http://www.religioustolerance.org/newage.htm, 3/10/07

10. Hanegraaff, "What Is the New Age Movement," The information was accessed through the following website: http://www. equip.org/.

Age author Fritjof Capra, is "a seamless web of vibrant, pulsating energy."[11] Because all reality is essentially one, man imagines himself capable of tapping into divine energy and experiencing godhood. This, indeed, seems to be the target towards which the most famous secular spokespersons of the New Age movement aim their ambitions. "Kneel to your own self," says Swami Muktananda, "Honor and worship your own being. God dwells within you as You!"[12]

According to Ken VanDyken, a research student of Postmodernism, many of the beliefs of New Agers have become the central identifying descriptors of Postmodernism. Consider these characteristics that, he says, mark our age:

- There are no universal truths
- All is subjective, objectivity is an illusion
- Uncritical acceptance of all beliefs
- They question the truthfulness of the representation of history
- The power of story telling is valued more than the power of the facts
- Reality is defined by images, visual and simulation is considered real
- Meaning is determined by one's cultural position, age, gender
- There is no distinction between good and bad, all is relative
- They question which God you believe in, not whether you believe in God
- Emphasize multiplicity, diversity, multi-paths, not linear thinking
- Relationships are more important than institutions

11. Burrows, "Americans Get Religion in the New Age," 19.
12. Hunt, *The Cult Explosion,* 106.

- Poly-sexual norms replace heterosexual norms
- Process and performance are more important than finished product

As Dave Hunt and T. H. McMahon convincingly demonstrate in their shocking book, *The Seduction of Christianity*, many evangelical churches, both in America and abroad, have begun to echo more and more of the sentiments of this syncretistic, pantheistic, and Eastern religious philosophy. Kenneth Copeland's bold assertion that we are gods, and Earl Paulk's teaching that God has begotten us as little gods in the same manner as dogs have puppies and cats have kittens,[13] illustrates with stunning poignancy the truth of Hunt and McMahon's observations.[14]

If godhood is the aspiration of many adherents of the New Age movement, how is it achieved? It's by way of enlightenment. "For Capra, history is not the story of humanity's fall into sin and its restoration by God's saving acts. History is the story of humanity's fall into ignorance and gradual ascent into enlightenment."[15]

13. See Hunt and McMahon, *Seduction*, 219.

14. Of course, the lie that people can become divine is as old as the bogus claims the serpent made to Eve in the Garden of Eden (see Genesis 3:1–4).

15. Burrows, *Americans Get Religion*, 18–19. Adherents of the New Age movement reflect the kind of mixed up thinking that existed among pagans living during the time of Paul. The apostle said these unbelievers "suppress the truth by their wickedness" (Romans 1:18). In particular, they reject the evidence of God's "eternal power and divine nature" (verse 20) evident through His creation and made "plain to them" (verse 19). Instead of glorifying the Lord as God and giving thanks to Him, "their thinking became futile and their foolish hearts were darkened" (verse 21). And, despite their claims to be wise, they were really fools (verse 22). Their moral deficiency and inclination toward evil was evident in their decision to worship idols made to look like mere people or lesser creatures in the world (verse 23). God,

"But," you might ask, "How can one become enlightened?" The New Agers' most common answer is that it comes through mental exercises that produce a heightened state of consciousness capable of creating its own future. By slipping into the consciousness of the cosmos, some New Age mystics claim extraordinary powers, including such marvels as the miraculous healing of terminal diseases and pre-programming children's behavior. Visualization and recitation of mantras[16] appear to be their most frequently used techniques.

It's amazing how even well-trained, biblically astute church leaders sometimes fall prey to these attempts at manipulating God. I am not surprised when someone like the hardened, vacant-eyed Taiwanese spirit medium who challenged me to a spiritual duel seeks supernatural insight and power via magical techniques. But I am shocked and distressed when those who should know better promote similar practices from the pulpit! How can one who understands that God blesses those who trust in Him claim that human mental projection, "positive thinking, positive speaking, and positive visualization are the keys to success?"[17]

God's forgiving grace and sustaining power are not antithetical to positive thoughts, words, and plans that are biblically conceived. But He is indeed opposed to mental projections that are intended to "create reality." God alone creates reality and acts in sovereign might. We ought never

---

in turn, judged them by giving them over to sexual impurity (verses 24–25), sexual perversion (verses 26–27), and a depraved mind (verse 28). This led to a host of evil deeds (verses 29–31) and spiritual death (verse 32).

16. A mantra is a special word or phrase that is thought to have spiritual power. See Lardie et al., *Concise Dictionary of the Occult and New Age,* 165.

17. Hunt and McMahon, *Seduction,* 16. See also Lardie et al., *Concise Dictionary of the Occult and New Age,* 277.

to suggest, as some prominent churchmen do, that through mind conditioning we can make the world what we want it to be.

There are preachers who encourage congregations to figure out what criteria God has adopted for the distribution of blessings. The goal is to manipulate the Lord to act on the basis of so-called "laws of success." Tragically, these ministers have veered from grace and set themselves over God. As they curl their white-knuckled fists toward heaven, they try to reduce Him to an idol. And once they feel in charge of this "god," they waste no time in assigning priorities for its attention. What they hope for often bears little resemblance to the hope of the gospel.

Some time ago, I heard a woman on the radio instruct her listeners how to get the things they wanted from God. She conjectured that negative thoughts by believers would cause God to withhold what He might have been about to give. "For example," she said, "God may have been about to drop the keys of the new car that you wanted into your hands, but because of the negative thought that flitted through your mind, He withdrew them until you display doubt-free faith for an acceptable period of time." She spoke of faith as mental staying power, which, because of its tenacity, is able to win exciting concessions from a reluctant God.

Another occasion when faith was misconstrued as a humanly released force was when a self-proclaimed "faith healer" who, having been denied his request of praying over a dying Christian leaned with arms uplifted in prayer against the wall of the adjacent hospital room to induce healing. His accusation against the devout family members was that their weak faith obstructed the energy of God. "How could he be right," troubled family members wondered, "when the same God the faith healer claims to represent is also the One we believe and trust? Could it really be that we are responsible for the death of our loved one?"

Faith, when seen as a force by which God can be managed, destroys hope. When with such "faith" the mouths of man-made "gods" spew great promises, lasting hope is never imparted. Rather, a wispy wish dances before the eyes and, like steam, vanishes when the heat rises or the pressure builds.

In contrast, faith, when understood as trust in the promises, will, and character of almighty God, builds rock-solid hope. True believers can be absolutely certain that God will fulfill all His gracious plans and carry them into the grandeur of His presence (Psalm 33:10–11; Job 42:2; Isaiah 46:10; Daniel 4:35). No longer do they live in a tottering house of cards of their own engineering, a house that could collapse not only from gales, but also from an unexpected gust. God is a Workman who always accomplishes what He sets out to do, and He builds lives according to His divinely ordained purpose (Matthew 7:24–27).

Hopeful believers thrill to hear God say, "For I know the plans I have for you . . . plans to prosper you and not to harm you, plans to give you a hope and a future" (Jeremiah 29:11). But believers are confused and misled when they are told that they should "tap into spiritual forces that can reverse our destiny and the destiny of those around us."[18] Positive thinking that focuses on man's power and glory, rather than God's, is at best seriously misdirected and at worst, utterly hopeless.

The Hope of Glory Diminished

Early church Christians were full of expectation and hope. As citizens of heaven, they waited eagerly for "a Savior from

18. Larson, "Hope—The Power for Your Future," 31.

there, the Lord Jesus Christ, who, by the power that enables him to bring everything under his control, will transform our lowly bodies so that they will be like his glorious body" (Philippians 3:20–21). As they waited for His appearing, they learned the self-control necessary "to say 'No' to ungodliness and worldly passions, and to live self-controlled, upright and godly lives in this present age" (Titus 2:12). They understood that the indwelling, transforming presence of God's Spirit was the hope of glory (Colossians 1:27).

Will those who follow the popular possibility thinking ministries of our day develop a longing and expectation similar to that of early Christians? I think not. For example, adherents of Robert Schuller's positive teaching will almost certainly miss out on true biblical hope. Because Schuller too radically tailors his message to meet the desires of his target audience (not because he himself misunderstands the hope of the gospel), his hearers receive an artificial, imitation hope.

The dichotomy between Schuller's personal grasp of hope and the adapted version that he presents to his audience is clarified by a letter dated November 25, 1985. In it, he describes biblical hope:

> God, who made me in His image, loves me unconditionally. He has come to me in Jesus Christ, lived for me, died for me, rose from death for me. Now, He gives me His Holy Spirit to share in His ministry to the world. . . . And I believe that one day; I shall be fully like Him. With this strong, rich hope, I can value myself the way God values me, pour my life into ministry, and leave the outcome confidently with the God of all grace. Hope is the engine that drives my ministry!

Despite his accurate personal understanding, Schuller's preaching reduces true hope. Schuller offers this defense for modifying the Bible's proclamation of hope:

> For the church to address the unchurched with a theocentric attitude *is to invite failure in mission* [emphasis mine]. The non-churched, who have no vital belief in a relationship with God, will spurn, reject, or simply ignore the theologian, church spokesperson, preacher, or missionary who approaches with Bible in hand, theology on the brain and the lips, and expects nonreligious persons to suspend their doubts and swallow the theocentric assertions as fact.[19]

Dennis Voskuil, in his book, *Mountains into Goldmines,* further explains Schuller's selection of sermon topics as follows:

> It is clear that Schuller views possibility thinking as a vehicle for success, generally understood in terms of this-worldly health, happiness, and prosperity. Those disturbed by this consistent emphasis upon earthly concerns must be reminded that Schuller begins from the point of human needs; to make an impact on the essentially secular and materialistic person, Schuller stresses what will catch his or her fancy. It is also important to remember that the basic thrust of Schuller's appeal is similar to that of nearly all evangelistic preachers: while they advertise eternal bliss, he advertises more immediate spiritual and emotional benefits. This is not to say that Schuller does not believe in the after-life. He is utterly orthodox on this point, but he does not stress it very much in his public ministry.

19. Schuller, *Self-Esteem: The New Reformation*, 12.

> Schuller is witnessing to an audience interested
> in immediate rather than long-range needs.
> They want a Christianity that bears fruit here
> and now.[20]

Irrespective of Schuller's laudatory objective, the gospel of hope cannot be faithfully preached without reference to the subjects he avoids. Preaching that conceals or minimizes the salient features of biblical hope misguides worshipers. They learn to major on the minors.

Schuller sometimes compares worshipers to "shoppers" in a "spiritual marketplace." Using this analogy, we must question the value of a cart full of self-esteem cosmetics (like those peddled by Schuller) with few, if any, of the essential life-surrendering, God-glorifying staples of the Christian faith. Phlegmatic church-goers rarely covet "products" crucial to spiritual life, but this is no reason for a preacher to remove them from his shelves, nor to replace them with inferior substitutes. Indeed, the preacher must expose their dangerous apathy and warn against it!

Replacing Schuller as the premier self-esteem preacher of our day Joel Osteen, the senior pastor of Lakewood Church in Houston, Texas, shares his version of optimism with millions every week. Although Osteen does not regard himself as a traditional preacher of positive thinking, it is clear that his seven steps to living at one's full potential are specifically designed to enable his listeners to shuck off negative thoughts and influence and replace them with thoughts that are happy, pretty, and self-satisfying.

Good titles of books inform readers what to expect between the covers. Osteen's title, *Your Best Life Now*, is a good title. It trumpets the exciting news that right now, through proven formulas, you can slip the best, brightest

20. Voskuil, *Mountains Into Goldmines*, 112.

and most fulfilling blessings from God's hands! Your best life can be n-o-w!

Sadly, this promising title reveals a pessimistic view of heaven. Our best life is not now! It is in eternal glory in the presence of God. The goodness and grace of God that we sample now is only a foretaste of the glory to come. Our "best life" is not merely to have the riches and pleasures of this world at our disposal, but to take all that we have and are and use them in the service of the King.

While Osteen's book contains many down-to-earth beneficial ideas about harmful self-depreciation, its main message is about positive mind control and how to get the things you want.

On the last page of his book, Osteen writes that he closes every international television broadcast by giving the audience an opportunity to make Jesus the Lord of their lives. In his appeal to make Jesus Lord of life he asks his listeners and readers to repent of sins and invite Jesus into their hearts.[21] I am glad he includes these words in his sermons and book. But, why are they just an addendum? Why are they like the tag along commercials behind a TV program-always there but disconnected from the program itself? Why aren't they central to hope and the future?

What is the goal of Christian hope to which you must point worshipers? It is the return of Jesus Christ and eternal life in the presence of our holy, almighty God! This is the goal for which every spiritually healthy heart throbs.

Old Testament saints dreamed of "dwelling in the house of the LORD forever" (Psalm 23:6). Ezekiel concluded his prophecy in anticipation of the establishment of the city named "THE LORD IS THERE" (Ezekiel 48:35). God Himself, and life in His presence, was their hope.

---

21. Osteen, *Your Best Life Now*, 310

New Testament saints, likewise, longed for perfected life in God's glorifying presence. They loved His light, for they were attracted to it (John 3:21). They strained their ears to hear the voice from the throne saying, "Now the dwelling of God is with men, and he will live with them. They will be his people and God himself will be with them and be their God. He will wipe away every tear from their eyes. There will be no more death or mourning or crying or pain, for the old order of things has passed away" (Revelation 21:3–4).

Preaching hope without emphasizing God's sacred presence, the resurrection of the dead, and the return of Christ is like talking about marriage without mentioning a spouse. Hope means heaven,[22] and heaven means God's presence. We cannot have biblical hope without longing to be with God.

This simple equation is missed almost entirely in Schuller's theological work, *Self-Esteem: The New Reformation.* In it, he discusses the Lord's Prayer and focuses almost entirely upon the glory of man, omitting the glory of God.

"How," you might wonder, "can one focus on his own esteem when the petitions under consideration ask for the hallowing of the Father's name, the coming of His kingdom, and the advancement of His will?" To Schuller's mind, this is simple. Since he asserts that God's honor and glory are promoted when our self-esteem grows, it follows that preaching self-esteem automatically results in praise to God. Schuller's assertion contains some truth. One of the pleasant realities of glory will be perfect honor and respect for everyone in it. And Schuller is right to encourage the

---

22. Namely, the perfection of the communion with God we have already begun to enjoy.

practice of proper respect for one another here and now as we make our way to glory.

Both Schuller's and Osteen's messages of hope are inadequate and insufficient in that they fail to announce the primary feature of heaven, that is, the attractive, holy presence of God! Since God's magnificent and awesome holiness is not clearly preached, sin, which is an affront to that holiness, is also avoided. Rather than boldly and positively declaring sin to be rebellion against God, it is presented in comfortable and acceptable terms as failure to esteem self and others and, thus, as failure to honor what God treasures.

This weak and shallow view of sin leads to confusion about our real condition before the face of God (Romans 3:23; 6:23). And I fear that this type of preaching may result in people going to hell with dignity! If the man on my street who follows such teaching suddenly died, he might expect to enter heaven because he values himself as positive thinking pastors recommend. But, if he were admitted to glory, I think he would be shocked to find God there!

As pastors and worship leaders, we must constantly beware of tailor-making messages to avoid any talk of moral depravity, guilt, and condemnation. When church leaders lock their attention on sermon appeal, their messages gradually adapt to the tastes of the listeners rather than serve their divinely revealed needs.[23] Response-driven leaders maintain that if the worship services seem too long, they should be shortened. If they are too formal or boring, they should be jazzed up. And if the services are too weighty, they should be purged of "old-fashioned authority, guilt trips, account-

23. Middleman, *The Market-Driven Church: The Worldly Influence of Modern Culture on the Church in America*, 18–19, 50–51, 116–117, 124–125.

ability, and moral absolutes."[24] The result is predictable—
"Christianity Lite," namely, everything you always wanted
in Christianity—and less![25]

Church growth experts identify this as a seeker-driven
approach to congregational worship. Bryan D. Spinks describes it as follows: "The sanctuary becomes a stage, the
minister becomes a talk-show host, and the congregation
becomes an audience."[26] Ministers feel pressured to operate
in this way because they fear that weekly attendance will
either level off or decline, with the added effect of eroding
their church's finances. In desperation, these pastors adopt a
purely pragmatic approach in which "the criterion is 'whatever works.'"[27]

David F. Wells considers this outlook to be a dressed
up form of modernity.[28] Self, rather than God, is on the
throne of one's life. The goal is no longer to be freed from
sin and pardoned from iniquity; rather, it is to have the
wounded psyche healed. The foremost objectives are not
the reverence of God and the betterment of others; instead,
an internalized form of spirituality is adopted in which the
central preoccupation becomes relieving one's "pains, ambi-
guities, and sense of loss."[29]

---

24. MacArthur, *Hard to Believe: The High Cost and Infinite Value
of Following Jesus*, 1.

25. Ibid., 1–2.

26. Spinks, "Worshiping the Lamb or Entertaining the Sheep?
Evaluating Evangelical Practice By the Reformed Principles of
Worship," 14.

27. Ibid.

28. Wells, "Introduction: The Word in the World," in *The
Compromised Church*, 30. See the corresponding analysis offered by
Middleman, *The Market-Driven Church: The Worldly Influence of
Modern Culture on the Church in America*, 44–48.

29. Wells, "Introduction: The Word in the World," 30. Jay Tolson
comes close to the mark when he states that modern evangelism is

Achieving personal wholeness, not growing more holy, becomes the all-consuming passion. In this worldly manner of thinking, scriptural truths give way to gut feelings, and the quest for personal gratification replaces the abandonment of sin. Achieving fame and fortune become a higher priority than remaining committed to Christ. Wells concludes that "worship in such contexts often has little or nothing to do with God."[30]

Such believers, rather than being "transformed by the renewing of [their] mind" (Romans 12:1), find themselves being conformed to "the pattern of this world." Likewise, they fail to realize that "friendship with the world is hatred toward God" (James 4:4) and that "the world and its desires" (I John 2:17) are passing away. This is a situation in which self, rather than the Savior, is the starting point and end goal of human existence.[31]

T. M. Moore captures the essence of these verses in this way: "In this case, [believers] will have compromised their callings as citizens of the kingdom of God, abandoned their distinctives as followers of Christ, and become absorbed into the miasma of self that is the dominant feature of postmodern society."[32] And what is the consequence? "Such an agenda can lead, on the one hand, to personal

characterized by its "strongly personalist and therapeutic tendencies, its market-savvy approaches to expanding the flock, and even a certain theological fuzziness." See "The New Old-Time Religion," *U.S. News & World Report,* Washington, D.C.: U.S. News and World Report, December 8, 2003. The information was accessed through the following website: http://www.usnews.com/.

30. Wells, "Introduction: The Word in the World," 31.

31. Middleman, *The Market-Driven Church: The Worldly Influence of Modern Culture on the Church in America,* 65, 106–107, 133, 136, 144–145.

32. Moore, *Redeeming Pop Culture: A Kingdom Approach,* 15.

disillusionment and social disarray . . . and, on the other hand, to the destruction of all meaning."[33]

The solution to this problem is a recommitment to a biblical worldview.[34] Regrettably, untold numbers of preachers throughout the U.S. have wandered far from this path. According to Gene Edward Veith, "only half of America's ministers hold to a biblical worldview."[35] What's worse, "even many who do aren't imparting it to their congregations." These pastors have forgotten Peter's injunction to be "shepherds of God's flock that is under your care" (1 Peter 5:2). They have also ignored Paul's exhortation to the Ephesian elders: "Keep watch over yourselves and all the flock of which the Holy Spirit has made you overseers. Be shepherds of the church of God, which he bought with his own blood" (Acts 20:28).

Pastor, if you want your church to grow, then resist the temptation to bow before the shrines of feel-good, positive thinking, New Age spirituality, and seeker-sensitive reenvisioning of the old fashioned gospel of grace. Proclaim to your people that true believers have more inner strength and fortitude than anyone else on earth. They know their Creator and realize that they bear His image. Thus, they should never regard themselves (as many unbelievers do) as "human trash"—poorly made, of inferior quality, and mentally or physically embarrassing. God made us! And the Lord is responsible for the quality of His products.

33. Ibid., 13.

34. This world-and-life view affirms Jesus as Lord, the rule of God over all things, the mission of the church through proclamation (or word) and action (or deed), the mandate of human beings to rule the world with God as His stewards, the importance of Christian education in all spheres of life, and the entire life of the believer as a divine vocation, a response to God's call to follow Christ.

35. Veith, "Stray Pastors," 25.

Because the Lord made us according to His design, we can hold our heads high and look eye-to-eye with others as equally valuable creations of God. No one should be ashamed because of how he or she was made. Furthermore, because we know and esteem our Redeemer as the One who purchases our salvation and cleanses our consciences, we find full relief from our burden of guilt. In Christ, we are completely forgiven and through Him we learn to forgive both others and ourselves (Ephesians 3:10; 4:32).

Believers view themselves as God's creation and Christ's re-creation. What confidence we have! And what worth, worth rooted entirely in the character and craftsmanship of God. Since God and His works are irreducible in value, so are we, the eternally precious children of our Father.

Only when we repent and believe do we realize our true worth. By turning to God in sorrow for sin and trusting Him for our redemption, we become esteemed by none other than God Himself! Isaiah expressed God's view regarding human worth in these words: "This is the one I [the LORD] esteem: he who is humble and contrite in spirit, and trembles at my word" (Isaiah 66:2).

Before the loving and gracious face of the Almighty, we truly "find ourselves." That is why human self-esteem, apart from the pardoning presence of the Lord, is God-repudiating self-glory. Thus, while Schuller is probably correct in his judgment that sinful people long for self-esteem, he is wrong in his contention that the universal aspiration for self-worth qualifies as the central or primary hope of the gospel.

In contrast to Schuller and others who diminish the gospel, faithful preachers of biblical hope are positive for the right reasons. They declare that where sin abounds, grace super-abounds (Romans 5:20–21). They are absolutely convinced that, because Christ arose, ascended to the Father's right hand, and will come again in power and great glory, our labor in the Lord is not in vain (I Corinthians 15:58).

Faithful preachers of biblical hope extend encouragement to the oppressed. They point them to the certain return of Jesus and invite participation in His coming glorious kingdom. Do you? What hope do you offer the troubled and discouraged? Is it the hope of the Bible or an inferior hope? The hope God offers us in Christ shines from eternity, illuminating the path to His sacred presence. Your aim as a preacher of hope is to clarify how, in Christ, the future invades the present.

CHAPTER FOUR

Incomplete Views of Hope (Part Two)

IN CHAPTER three, we saw how "positive thinking" and "New Age perspectives" tend to reduce the hope of the gospel to a mere shadow of what it is in Scripture. When preaching concretizes the object of hope only in terms of material possessions and pleasant experiences for the here and now, it does so at the expense of what the Bible considers far more real and valuable, namely, the unseen and the eternal.

Other villains that thwart biblical hope are dispensational premillennialism and liberalism. Dispensational premillennialism diminishes authentic biblical hope by too closely tracing the finger of God in history, and by focusing more on the penultimate than the ultimate.[1] And, liberalism extinguishes hope by regarding the Parousia and resurrection as myths. Let's explore further how these two perspectives of end times events offer incomplete notions of hope.

Dispensationalism: Saboteur of Hope?

Those who sympathize with dispensational premillennialism[2] might regard as ludicrous the suggestion that it sabo-

---

1. I am limiting this discussion to dispensational premillenialism because its proponents tend to hang hope on an intricate sequence of events, on the rapture and the millennium, more than on the eternal kingdom.

2. For an examination of the historical background and theological

tages hope. After all, dispensationalists feel they hold the most literal, biblical, historical, and forward-looking view of eschatology.[3] According to dispensationalists, their view is also realistic. Unlike postmillennialists,[4] they do not expect the world to get better as history progresses.

Because dispensational premillennialism has a comprehensive yet specific perspective of the future, it has great power to engender hope. Furthermore, it has been used of God to bring many unbelievers to Christ. When people are told that current world events are predicted on the pages of Scripture and that God will shortly intervene in this world to bring it to His desired end, they sit up and take note. For that reason, the popular *Left Behind* series by Tim LaHaye

underpinnings of dispensationalism, see Poythress, *Understanding Dispensationalists*, 1994; Mathison, *Dispensationalism: Rightly Dividing the People of God?* 1995; and Gerstner, *Wrongly Dividing the Word of Truth: A Critique of Dispensationalism*, 2000. These authors note that classic dispensationalists maintain a sharp distinction between Israel and the church. All of the prophecies regarding ethnic, national, political Israel (for example, those pertaining to the messianic kingdom) are understood to apply specifically and directly to that entity and not to the church. Common teachings resulting from this view include: the secret rapture of the saints; seven years of tribulation; and the literal thousand year reign of Christ on earth.

3. Eschatology may be defined as the "doctrine of the 'last things' (Gr. *eschata*), in relation either to human individuals (comprising death, resurrection, judgment, and the afterlife) or to the world" (Howard-Snyder, "Eschatology," in *Evangelical Dictionary of Theology*, 386).

4. "Postmillennialism is that view of the last things which holds that the kingdom of God is now being extended in the world through the preaching of the gospel and the saving work of the Holy Spirit in the hearts of individuals, that the world eventually is to be Christianized and that the return of Christ is to occur at the close of a long period of righteousness and peace commonly called the millennium" (Boettner, *The Meaning of the Millennium: Four Views,* 63). Postmillennialism is also the field of eschatology that dispensational premillennialism tried to displace at the end of the nineteenth century.

and Jerry B. Jenkins[5] has been an unusually effective evangelistic tool. By some estimates, these novels, whose plot revolves around the rapture,[6] have sold tens of millions of copies.[7]

There are other reasons why it may seem ridiculous to charge that dispensational premillennialism dispels hope. For instance, it purports to unlock many of the mysteries of the Bible and seems to give adherents a clearheaded grasp of the future. I well remember the aura of excitement in a dispensational colleague's voice when he showed me the expansive end time charts displayed in the front of his church. He spoke as though hope and his charts were synonymous, and he pitied those for whom the secrets of the ages were a closed book.

But is the detailed dispensational schedule of the fulfillment of end time events really the means God has designed for the church to become more hopeful? The answer is *no*. The reason for saying this is straightforward. In the New Testament, hope is not stimulated by setting dates and charting their supposed "fulfillment," but by urging continual observance of the signs of the times and preparation for the Parousia, judgment, and eternal kingdom. When hope is generated by trying to figure out where one is on the last-day's itinerary, it is misplaced and is likely to end in disappointment and despair.

---

5. LaHaye and Jenkins, *Left Behind Series.*

6. The word "rapture" comes from the Latin term *rapio*, which means "caught up." Theologians use "rapture" to "refer to the church being united with Christ at his second coming" (Clouse, "Rapture of the Church," in *Evangelical Dictionary of Theology*, 983).

7. Safer, "Rise of the Righteous Army," *60 Minutes*, February 8, 2004.

The Signs of the Times

The "signs of the times" (Matthew 16:3) are some of dispensational premillennialists' main points of reference for determining proximity to the last day. These signs, they believe, are clear and precise indications of Jesus' immanent return.[8] What are these signs? According to I. M. Haldeman, former pastor of the First Baptist Church of New York (1911), they include the following:

> The widespread preparation for war, the downgrade in the Protestant church, the upgrade in the Roman church, the accumulation of wealth in the hands of the few, the increase of knowledge [in the context, Haldeman means science], running to and fro—rapid transit and rapid flight—the multiplication of human inventions, the expanding cry that the voice of the people is the voice of God [in the context, Haldeman means socialism], the return of the Jew to his own land, the stealthy but steady strides of pestilence and the sudden grip of famine . . . everywhere heart failure mixed with bold boasting and unconcealed defiance of God—what are these but the very signs pictured in the Word of God as antedating the advent of Christ.[9]

In 1972, Tim LaHaye cited the following signs of the times in his book, *The Beginning of the End:* world war started by two nations, famines, pestilence, many earthquakes at once, Israel becoming a nation, rise of Russia, apostasy, occultism, ecumenical church, capital and labor conflict,

---

8. Jesus' immanent return means that it could happen at any moment without warning.

9. Haldeman, *Signs of the Times,* 30–31.

moral breakdown, one world government, increase in travel and knowledge, and scoffers.[10]

A more recent prophet of signs is Morris Cerullo. In his 2004 video titled *America in Prophecy*,[11] Cerullo asserts that God gave him a revelation of end-time events pertaining to the U.S. and the world. He claims that he has a divine mandate to sound the alarm across the entire globe against the impending attacks of secularism and paganism.

Along with Cerullo, many other dispensational premillennialists emphasize the following signs of the times: the U.S. is in a major prophetic cycle that is parallel to ancient Israel; in the last days the European economic union will become the revived form of the culture and peoples of the Roman Empire; in the end times this European commonwealth will form a peace treaty with the modern state of Israel; China and other Asiatic peoples are the "kings from the East" of Revelation 16:12; the U.S. is the mystery Babylon of Revelation 17–18; at the end of the age Russia will attack America from the north (Jeremiah 50; Ezekiel 38–39); and the rapture could occur at any time, leaving America little more than seven years away from the battle of Armageddon.

Declarations such as these are supported by references to contemporary historical events to substantiate the claim that America is in the last times.[12] It is alleged that we live within the generation when Jesus must return. LaHaye, in fact, is even more specific. He says the clock of the end times began ticking in 1914.

10. LaHaye, *The Beginning of the End*, 162–163.

11. Cerullo, *America in Prophecy: Sound the Alarm!*

12. Theologians often use the phrases "last days(s)," "latter days," and "last times" synonymously to refer to the end of all things inaugurated by Jesus' return. Morris, "Last Days(s), Latter Days, Last Times," in *Evangelical Dictionary of Biblical Theology*, 464–467.

The problem with using signs to pinpoint the exact time (or even the exact generation) of Jesus' return is two-fold. First, we might be inaccurate in our selection and interpretation of the signs, as William Miller was when he predicted that Christ would come back between March 21, 1943 and March 21, 1944, thus misrepresenting God. Miller and others prove how hazardous it is to be specific about the exact application of prophetic and apocalyptic references.[13] Second, Jesus condemns all efforts at pinpointing the date of His return.[14] During His earthly ministry, even He did not know the day or the hour (Matthew 24:36).

Does dating generations or years instead of the exact moment of the Parousia itself help us avoid making mistakes and violating our Lord's teaching? Certainly not! Jesus' intent was that we stop trying to pick the dates of God's inexorable calendar and concentrate our intentions upon *always* being ready for His return (II Peter 3:11–14). Then, if Jesus' comes today (which is possible) or a thousand years

13. The word "apocalypse" derives its name from the Greek term for "revelation" (*apokalypsis*). The Book of Daniel in the Old Testament and the Book of Revelation in the New Testament are familiar examples of apocalyptic literature. The *Dictionary of Biblical Imagery* has this generalized comment regarding biblical genre: "Though apocalypse may be considered a subgenre of prophecy, the two literary styles are sufficiently different to merit calling them separate genres. Prophecy speaks to those who have backslidden and begs them to repent; apocalyptic speaks to the faithful and urges them to persevere. Prophecy announces God's judgment of sin on the local scale using natural means; apocalyptic announces a coming cataclysm when the whole earth will be destroyed. Prophecy records its message in poetry; apocalyptic in narrative accounts of visions . . . Prophecy promises restoration and future blessing; apocalyptic an unexpected divine visitation that will result in a new heaven and new earth." Ryken, *Dictionary of Biblical Imagery*, 35–36.

14. For a helpful discussion of the signs of the times, see Hoekema, *The Bible and the Future*, 137–163.

from now, the signs will have served their God-ordained purpose.

It is clear that when the signs of the times are thought of as referring exclusively to the end-time, and as instruments for gauging how close we are to the Parousia, we will begin to make errors in judgment. But, if they are viewed as having a past, present, and future reference, as they do in Matthew 16:1–4, we will not make date-setting mistakes and will remain alert for Jesus' impending return.

Preachers of hope must be wary. Dating future events, shedding biblical mystery, and mapping out the future as if it were prewritten history is tantalizing. It draws crowds and sells books. But it clashes with Jesus' instruction, causes believers to pin their hope on the wrong events, and sets them up for despair.

In a short end-times date-setting booklet that I received some time ago, Edgar C. Whisenant said that "the harvest of wicked non-believers starts at sunset September 20, 1988, the start of the Day of Atonement, and continues for seven years." He further explained that this is "the end of the Church age, the exact end of the age spoken of in Matthew 13:39." Furthermore, Whisenant declared, "Using Rosh-Hashanah as the date of the Rapture of the church, the dates of the remaining end-time events can now be found. The Rapture will occur sometime during the period of Rosh-Hashanah, between sunset, September 11 and sunset, September 13."[15]

If we were convinced that Whisenant's interpretation was accurate, we would necessarily despair when we woke up on the morning of the fourteenth. And if he had been correct and we failed to be raptured on the dates he specified, we would conclude that we were going to be included in the "harvest of wicked unbelievers." If we did

15. Whisenant, *On Borrowed Time*, 6 and 9.

not surmise, on the basis of Whisenant's prognostications that we were hopeless and helpless, it is quite likely that we would become complacent and apathetic about our Lord's return. We might well decide that every interpreter of biblical prophecy is a phony. Or, worst yet, we may even judge God's Word as being false. Any such outcome is hopeless!

The Apostle's Example

The apostles lived and ministered in troubled times. Danger was continually knocking at their doors. They needed hope and encouragement. How did they find it? Was it by combing prophecy, piecing it together like a cosmic puzzle, and displaying elaborate charts? No!

What the apostles did was to point over and over again to the foundational truths of Jesus' resurrection, His ascension, His reign at the Father's right hand, Jesus' Parousia, His judgment of the wicked, and the eternal glory awaiting the redeemed. Beyond that the apostles did not go. No more was needed for hope, even during episodes of intense persecution experienced by first century believers (Revelation 1:9).

We should follow the apostles' example. I am not saying that you should never teach anything about the intricacies of prophecy or show its relationship to current events. Nor am I saying that you should avoid altogether the topic of the sequence of future events. What I do mean is that you should be careful not to tie the hope of believers to your particular rendition of the precise details and dates of the eschatological agenda. Rather, your preaching should direct your members to the fundamentals of the faith, as the apostles did. Solid hope is built on absolutes of God's Word, not on humanly contrived possibilities!

Make the Ultimate the Ultimate

The ultimate hope of believers is the eternal kingdom of God, not the rapture or the millennium. Yet, in Christian dispensational premillennial literature, I have found an alarming neglect of attention to this ultimate hope. What is of primary concern to many of these authors is the process and the sequence, rather than the eternal glory of God's kingdom.

By way of example, Tim LaHaye, in *The Beginning of the End*, almost completely ignores "the end" toward which "the beginning" points. Hal Lindsey is guilty of the same oversight in *The Late Great Planet Earth*. Similarly, in *The Terminal Generation*, though Lindsey speaks in a moving and powerful way about the hope of eternal life in the face of death, he stumbles in the last chapter. There he discusses the ultimate hope by fixing on the rapture and on his conviction that ours is the terminal generation. Jack Van Impe, in his book, *Everything You Always Wanted to Know About Prophecy But Didn't Know Who to Ask!* likewise focuses on the rapture and the millennium. In fact, he makes no mention of eternal life in the presence of the Lord.

How sad when the precursor to the finale is given the status of the culmination. Jesus' return to earth to raise the dead and call believers to be with Him is obviously important and exciting. In fact, it is the *focus* of biblical hope. But the millennium, although it is real and must be taken seriously, remains penultimate.

Accentuating and elevating that which precedes the end often results in the conclusion being overlooked. It diverts attention from the eternal to the temporary. That is a serious mistake, for it not only veers from the scriptural pattern, but also neglects the powerful impetus for holiness that the eternal provides. If you want to preach hope as the Bible presents it, preach the ultimate as the ultimate.

Liberalism—Reducer of Hope

We have seen how dispensational premillennialism detracts from the real hope of the gospel by turning attention away from what is essential. In contrast, liberalism[16] diminishes hope by eliminating or redefining essentials.

As was the case with dispensational premillennialism, liberalism did not intend to destroy hope. Rather, it had an "apologetic, pastoral, and missionary purpose." According to David Holwerda, the intent was to rescue Christianity from obsolete and misleading language as well as from dependence upon any worldview, and make it understandable and acceptable to the modern scientific mind. The task liberal theology set for itself was to see "that the gospel was not rejected for the wrong reasons."[17]

But liberal theology failed to accomplish its rescue of the gospel. Instead, it gutted the gospel and, in the process, shielded the world from being confronted by the true claims of Christ. When does one leave off removing the offense of the gospel and begin removing the gospel itself? This is the question we must ask as we look at liberal ideas regarding hope.

16. J. Gresham Machen was correct when he stated as follows the question that modern, naturalistic liberalism (which arose in the early 1900's) attempts to answer: "What is the relation between Christianity and modern culture; may Christianity be maintained in a scientific age?" See Machen, *Christianity and Liberalism*, 6. Also, see Pierard, "Liberalism, Theological," in *Evangelical Dictionary of Theology*, 682–685.

17. Holwerda, "The Challenge of Rudolf Bultmann," *The Reformed Journal*, 7. This statement about Rudolf Bultmann summarizes, I believe, the basic motivation of the entire liberal movement.

Alternative to Traditional Christian Hope

The alternative that nineteenth century liberal theology offered to traditional Christian hope tended to focus more and more on "the historical rather than the ultimate future."[18] One of the most influential early nineteenth century liberal theologians was Friedrich Schleiermacher (1768–1834). For Schleiermacher, the essence of religion was the feeling of God-consciousness.[19] Therefore, according to Schleiermacher, hope for the future meant the growth of the community in which God-consciousness was at its highest level, namely, the church. Although he did believe that human personality survived bodily death, Schleiermacher regarded the prophetic doctrines of the last things as largely symbolic of the ascent toward or possession of ultimate perfection.

A generation later, spurred on by "the anti-supernatural and anti-transcendental approach" of writers such as Ferdinand Christian Bauer (1792–1860) and David Friedrich Strauss (1808–1874), liberal theologians from Albrecht Ritschl (1822–1899) to Adolph VonHarnach (1851–1930) increasingly shifted "the focus of Christian hope towards a this-worldly theology of human progress."[20]

These theologians did not totally abandon the hope of heaven; but they ridiculed miracles, mysticism, and theologies of feeling and religious experience, while at the same time accentuating Christian ethics.

18. Hebblethwaite, *The Christian Hope*. 109. My analysis of the position of liberal theologians regarding hope is largely a summary of Hebblethwaite's excellent work.

19. Schleiermacher maintained that, "rather than religious experience growing out of doctrinal expressions or ecclesiastical life, religion itself was posited as the unique, primal experience of human existence" (Hoffecker, "Schleiermacher, Friedrich Daniel Ernst," in *Evangelical Dictionary of Theology*, 1065).

20. Hebblethwaite, *The Christian Hope*, 114.

"Liberal scholars recast Jesus as the supreme teacher of ethics rather than as the incarnate Son of God who was born of a virgin, who died an atoning death of cosmic significance, and who was raised bodily from the dead and ascended into heaven. These supernatural elements of the biblical portrait were rejected, and in their place was substituted the moralist Jew who advocated a kingdom of values and social responsibility."[21]

For Ritschl and VonHarnach, hope centered in the progressively realized ethical kingdom of God on earth.[22] To liberals, the Fatherhood of God, the brotherhood of man, and the infinite value of the human soul epitomized the Christian faith.

What effect does this perspective have on hope? It practically eliminates it. That sad fact is never more obvious than when liberal pastors make funeral arrangements for and deliver eulogies to their parishioners. These ministers reach far back into the deceased loved one's past as they deliver their tribute, but they have no basis upon which to reach forward in hope. Memorial songs and messages at these funerals often have a vain and secular cadence. At a critical moment that calls for biblical hope, liberal preaching leans backward rather than forward to a future secured in and through the risen and ascended Christ.

Dependence upon human achievement is a shallow and shortsighted ground for hope. Claims that the ethical kingdom of God will be realized on earth rather than in heaven are clearly unrealistic. Therefore, history of religion[23]

21. Sproul, *The Last Days According to Jesus*, 20.

22. Hebblethwaite, *The Christian Hope*, 114.

23. The phrase "history of religion" refers to an "influential movement among German academic theologians and biblical

theologians such as Johannes Weiss (1863–1914) and Albert Schweitzer (1875–1965) began to teach that the kingdom is an apocalyptic realm that will be inaugurated by God at the end of history.[24]

Based on an analysis of Jewish apocalyptic literature, Schweitzer believed that Jesus was a deluded fanatic who threw Himself sacrificially upon the crushing wheel of history in a desperate effort to bring in the kingdom. Although Jesus failed to establish His kingly reign as He had hoped, Schweitzer believed that Jesus succeeded in generating a forward-looking, self-renouncing spirit in this world as it awaits the Parousia.[25] Despite the continued popularity of Schweitzer's views, his understanding of the person and work of Christ must be rejected as unbiblical.

A contemporary of Schweitzer, Rudolf Bultmann (1884–1976) believed that the essence of Christian hope could be realized only by husking the true intent of the gospel of its heavy wrapping of myth:

> The eschatology of the Bible, especially that of the apocalyptic writings, according to Bultmann, was clearly mythological in form. Parousia, resurrection, the end of the world, heaven and

scholars stretching from about 1890 till 1930" (Yarbrough, "History of Religion School," in *Evangelical Dictionary of Theology*, 59). Adherents maintain that "Christianity definitely did not arise out of organic links with Old Testament history and view points; rather, pagan religions provided decisive impetus. Earlier Christianity was syncrestistic in nature in vital aspects." They also embrace a "'purely historical' approach which by definition [rules] out the presence of the theological (divinely revealed or transcendentally caused) within the historical."

24. Ladd, *The Gospel of the Kingdom*, 15.

25. See Price, "Schweitzer, Albert," in *New Dictionary of Theology*, 623–624.

> hell were all mythological ideas in the sense of
> ways of representing the eternal and the beyond
> in vivid this-worldly picture-language. Their
> existential meaning was not some future series
> of events but rather the ever-present possibility
> of an end to my worldly, inauthentic existence,
> and a beginning to the authentic life of faith.[26]

What remained when Bultmann finished this husking? It was only the encounter of the moment "between the word of God and the faith of the individual."[27] What meager treasures of hope, indeed! Even if Bultmann were totally correct, it seems hope would have been better served by allowing the gospel to remain encased in myth!

I well remember a "missionary" in Taiwan who was a brilliant proponent of Bultmann's view. This person loved to argue with others and tried to back them into theological corners. Sharp as he was in debate, however, he could not dress up death and make it attractive. Theology without a historical resurrection is a house of cards that collapses at death (I Corinthians 15:14).

C. H. Dodd (1884–1973), a British New Testament scholar, who was contemporary with Scheweitzer and Bultmann, was another influential interpreter of eschatology. Dodd believed "that Paul's early career is marked by an apocalyptic structure of thought (I Thessalonians) that he gradually abandoned because of his growing insight into the meaning of the Christ-myth as the 'realization' of the kingdom of God in history and because of the obstacles future apocalyptic produced for Paul's gentile mission." Dodd also thought "the stage of Paul's maturity is reached in Ephesians

26. Hebblethwaite, *The Christian Hope*, 139.
27. Ibid., p. 140.

where the apocalyptic consummation of history is displaced by the church as the divine commonwealth on earth."[28]

Another modern perspective of eschatology that we must mention is that of Jürgen Moltmann (born 1926). Troubled by the fact that eschatology was not given its proper place in theology, Moltmann set out to show that it was the central motif in all of God's dealings with humanity.

> According to Moltmann, eschatology had become nothing more than the sterile teaching of death and dying, rather than the living, vital hope which is supposed to rise out of the inherent contradiction between present and future. End-time events such as the second coming, the last judgment, and the resurrection of the dead were relegated to some future last day, divorced from our experience and thus robbed of their critical, guiding hope which has an impact on the present. As a result, eschatology developed as a kind of appendix to theology, taking up a barren existence at the end of systematic theology. Eschatology, however, was never intended to be the end of anything, but rather the beginning. It is in its essence the doctrine of a living hope in the future.[29]

Moltmann believed that humankind and history have a purpose far beyond the existential moment.[30] Having suffered the savagery of Hitler's army, and the disillusionment of Atheistic Marxism, Moltmann rallied the church to engage in responsible social and political action. In this

---

28. Beker, *Paul's Apocalyptic Gospel: The Coming Triumph of God*, 66.

29. Hesselgrave and Rommen, *Contextualization*, 42.

30. Bauckham, "Moltmann, Jürgen," in *New Dictionary of Theology*, 439–440.

way he exhorted the church to "be Christ" to the world and introduce to the world the future God has for it.

While legitimately stimulating the church to social action Moltmann did not fully escape liberal influence. He yielded to it by giving an unbalanced emphasis to the historical future over the ultimate future, and by construing the end-time more as an idea than as an actuality. Thus, "for Moltmann, the future which beckons us has hardly any substance."[31]

The views of Marcus J. Borg, Hundere Distinguished Professor of Religion and Culture at Oregon State University, are the last to which I call your attention. In his book, *The Heart of Christianity: Rediscovering a Life of Faith*, Borg discusses what he sees as the core or essence of the Christian faith and what it means to be a Christian in a time of change.[32]

Borg labels the theological views espoused by evangelical Christianity as an "earlier paradigm."[33] He considers this approach to be offensive and filled with unbelievable doctrines that should be jettisoned.[34] The replacement Borg presents is what he calls an "emerging paradigm" or a "second way of seeing Christianity."[35] He notes that this

31. Berkhof, *Well-Founded Hope*, 15.

32. M. J. Borg, *The Heart of Christianity: Rediscovering a Life of Faith*, xi, 1.

33. Ibid., pp. xii, 2. By paradigm, Borg means a "*comprehensive way of seeing*, a way of seeing a 'whole'" (p. 4; italics are his). He also describes a paradigm as a "large interpretive framework that shapes how everything is seen, a way of constellating particulars into a whole."

34. Ibid., pp. 18, 43–44, 82.

35. Ibid. On page 6 of his work, Borg states that the "emerging paradigm has been visible for well over a hundred years." A similar statement can be found on page 13. Remarks such as these support my contention that his approach to Christianity reflects the viewpoint of Protestant liberalism.

approach resulted from the contact of Christianity with "science, historical scholarship, religious pluralism, and cultural diversity." For him it is a "different way of seeing Christianity, one that takes seriously both the Christian tradition and who we have become."[36]

Borg offers a clear summary of the differences between evangelical Christianity and his postmodern[37] version.[38] Instead of seeing the Bible as a divinely inspired and authoritative document, it is a human product in which people recorded how they responded to an encounter with the divine. Scripture is no longer interpreted in a literal and factual way; rather, the text is understood to be filled with stories and myths. In its function, the Bible does not reveal doctrinal truths and moral absolutes; instead, it contains material that is sacramental and metaphorical in character. Lastly, the emphasis of the Christian life is not to believe the truth, get saved, and thereby have an assured hope of life in heaven; rather, it is to be transformed in this life through a relationship with God.

Borg's emerging paradigm repackages postmodern liberalism, exalts self above the Savior, and makes people, rather than the Lord, the center of existence. In this way of thinking, the Bible is humanity's witness to God, not God's special revelation to humanity. Literal facts recorded in the

36. Ibid., p. xiii.

37. As B. E. Benson notes in his article titled "Postmodernism" (*Evangelical Dictionary of Theology*, 939–945), it is difficult to describe all the nuances of this way of thinking. Nevertheless, there are broad aspects of postmodernism worth mentioning. For instance, truth and morals are relative and in a constant process of development and growth. Also, there is no such thing as propositional declarations, only changing metaphors and vague impressions of reality. Furthermore, life is always in a process of "becoming." In fact, this never-ending dynamic is seen as the defining core of existence.

38. Borg, *The Heart of Christianity: Rediscovering a Life of Faith*, pp. 7–15.

Bible, according to Borg, may be set aside for impressions, symbols, and ideas.[39] In respect to the nature and character of God, he is not understood to be self-existent, eternal, and unchanging, and is not thought to be distinct and separate from the world. Instead, He is declared to be "the More" and "ultimate reality" whose essence is panentheistic. In this way of thinking, the mysterious, all-encompassing presence called "God" inhabits the universe in the same way that a human soul inhabits the body.[40]

Borg maintains that Jesus is not God the Son, who became incarnate by being virginally conceived and born. Rather, He was an extraordinary human being whom people down through the centuries have regarded as: a Jewish mystic; a healer; a teacher of wisdom; a prophet who criticized the social, economic, and political injustices of His day; and the initiator of a compelling religious movement.[41] While Borg believes that Jesus was executed, he does not think Jesus literally died for our sins and that He is the exclusive way to the Father. Instead, Jesus is a "metaphor of God" who makes known what the divine is like. Furthermore, Jesus is not the Savior of the world, but a prism through whom we can catch a glimpse of God.[42]

According to Borg the doctrine of the resurrection is not the central truth of Christianity. The factuality of the empty tomb, he says, is unimportant. Instead, he places greater significance on the figurative meaning of Easter, which he asserts is that "you won't find Jesus in the land of the dead."[43] Because Borg has adopted a thoroughly human-centered, time-bound view of Scripture, faith, and

39. Ibid., pp. 45–46, 59–60.
40. Ibid., pp. 65–70.
41. Ibid., pp. 83, 89–91.
42. Ibid., pp. 91, 96–97.
43. Ibid., p. 55.

the key teachings of Christianity, he offers people no future hope of glory.[44]

Hope without Substance

As well intentioned as these modern substitutes for traditional Christian hope may be, they envision a desperately impoverished future for believers. Either they reduce the Messiah to a mistaken zealot or they pare down the promises of Scripture to a few residual truths that primarily have meaning for the here and now. In either case, eternal life in the presence of the Lord of glory is relinquished.

Whenever I read or hear preaching that relates only to this life, I think of the Book of Ecclesiastes. Everything is completely meaningless, Solomon declared, unless we remember the end to which life is leading (1:2). In light of God's eternal plan, we should fear Him and keep His commandments for, "God will bring every deed into judgment, including every hidden thing, whether it is good or evil" (12:13–14).

Must we who live in this scientific age give up so much to read the Bible accurately? The answer is "no"! To think in terms of heaven is not obsolete and mythical. Moderns as well as ancients can understand the concepts of God and of heaven and hell. Indeed, they must! God has written knowledge of His power and divinity into the fabric of every human soul (Romans 1:1–20). Even trigonometry and calculus do not erase this fundamental spiritual perception.

Machen was right in his contention that liberalism is not a *refined* gospel—it is *another* gospel (Galatians 1:6–9):

---

44. The basis for this last statement is found in Borg's comments about salvation and the afterlife (pp. 171–184). In particular, he rejects the notion of the redeemed abiding eternally with God in heaven. He regards salvation as the *present* transformation of self and society (p. 225).

> It is sometimes said that as Christians we may attend to what Christ does now for every Christian rather than to what He did long ago in Palestine. But the evasion involves a total abandonment of the Christian faith. If the saving work of Christ were confined to what He does now for every Christian, there would be no such thing as a Christian gospel—an account of an event which put a new face on life. What we should have left would be simply mysticism, and mysticism is quite different from Christianity. It is the connection of the present experience of the believer with an actual historic appearance of Jesus in the world which prevents our religion from becoming mysticism and causes it to be Christianity.[45]

If, in your preaching, you offer a this-worldly social gospel in place of the creation-restoring and redemptive gospel, the hope which you wish to present will be lost. To preach hope is to declare good news about what has happened in history and about what will take place in the world to come. It is to declare a physically resurrected Lord who now reigns at God's right hand and who will come again in power and great glory.

Proclamation of a hope that is off-centered, like that of dispensational premillenialism, eventually wobbles and self-destructs. And, preaching a hope devoid of biblical essentials, as liberalism does, is meaningless and false (I Corinthians 15:14). But proclamation of hope that announces the return of the risen, eternally reigning King, Jesus Christ our Lord, extends the encouragement you and your congregation need (I Thessalonians 4:13–18).

---

45. Machen, *Christianity and Liberalism*, 120.

CHAPTER FIVE

Preaching the Hope
of the Kingdom of God

"THE KINGDOM of God is advancing; and so is the kingdom of Satan—to its day of judgment! The gates of hell are giving way. Christ is already enthroned. His kingdom is emerging and His gathering church is looking forward to His spectacular appearance."

Does this sound like *your* preaching? Or is the tone of your sermons much more subdued and "realistic," more like the litany of tragedy recorded in your daily newspaper? If you preach, as some suggest, "with a newspaper in one hand and the Bible in the other," you might be inclined to focus on the battering of the church more than on the battering of the kingdom of darkness. Headlines from around the nation—San Diego, Portland, Chicago, and Washington, D.C.—report much more crime and criticism than love and good will. Therefore, it is understandable that some preachers portray the church as hanging on by tooth and nail rather than advancing in victory.

Which kingdom does your preaching depict as winning? Which is advancing to victory and which is losing ground? Powerful preaching of hope does not confront Satan's realm with whimpering fear. It boldly challenges ungodly philosophies and practices and confidently announces the victory of the reigning Monarch of all the earth!

People bombarded with the bad news of drugs, AIDS, homicides, and scandal crave the good news of God's kingdom. They want to hear that Satan's power has been broken and his faltering kingdom is hemmed in by God's expanding rule (Luke 10:18–19; Romans 16:20; Hebrews 2:14–15). They are eager for you to tell them that Christ, who reigns as King, is already governing everything for the sake of His church (Ephesians 1:19–23). When you announce the kingdom of God, you dispel the myth that Satan is omnipotent and that his darkness is impenetrable. As a preacher of the gospel of hope, you are ordained by God to set earth's bad news in the light of heaven's good news, the good news of the burgeoning kingdom of God!

The kingdom of God is certainly one of the most important and pervasive hope-building themes in the Bible. It appears with the call of Abram (Abraham) in Genesis 12:1–3 and expands until it includes people of every tribe, language, and race in Revelation 5:9–10. The divine kingdom progresses from earth to heaven, from shadow to reality, and from the tabernacle to the "Most Holy Place" in God's perfect presence. For believers who live in these "last days" before their King is revealed in glory, anticipation becomes intense, like the restlessness of a child on Christmas Eve and like the suspense of first-time parents in the delivery room (Romans 8:22–23). Has your preaching produced this sense of expectation in your congregation?

The Nature of the Kingdom of God

Although the kingdom of God was the central theme of Jesus' teaching, neither He nor the apostles, specifically defined it.[1] So, it may seem presumptuous or unnecessary to

---

1. Rather than defining the kingdom, Jesus used parables to describe and illustrate it.

offer a definition here; but we must do so in order that the teaching of the kingdom might serve as a resource of hope.

What is the kingdom of God? It is the Lord's rule (or reign) for the purpose of redemption.[2] This definition emphasizes two characteristics of the kingdom. First, God rules; and second, His rule is spiritual (in other words, has saving intention). Let's examine these two aspects further.

First, Scripture gives ample evidence that God's kingdom implies His rule.[3] In Exodus 19:5–6, God told Moses to promise the people of Israel that, "if you obey Me fully . . . then out of all nations you will be my treasured possession. Although the whole earth is mine, you will be for me a kingdom of priests and a holy nation" (I Peter 2:9–11).

Israel's calling as a kingdom of priests depended upon its willingness to obey, to be under God's rule. The Israelites forgot this truth and began to act as though their favored status as a covenant people would continue even if they ignored God. They believed that the kingdom of Israel would always be equivalent to the kingdom of God.

The relationship between God's kingdom and His rule is also obvious in the words of the Lord's Prayer, "your kingdom come, your will be done" (Matthew 6:10).

2. This definition, of course, is not applicable to the period before the Fall, when God's rule was uncontested.

3. For helpful discussions on the kingdom of God as His rule, see the following: Caragounis, "Kingdom of God/Heaven," in *Dictionary of Jesus and the Gospels*, 417–430; Gaffin, "Kingdom of God," in *New Dictionary of Theology*, 367–369; Goldsworthy, "Kingdom of God," in *New Dictionary of Biblical Theology*, 615–620; Hoekema, *The Bible and the Future*, 44–45; Kreitzer, "Kingdom of God/Christ," in *Dictionary of Paul and His Letters*, 525–526; Ladd, *The Gospel of the Kingdom*, 11, 19–23; Ladd, "Kingdom of Christ, God, Heaven," in *Evangelical Dictionary of Theology*, 657–660; Stein, "Kingdom of God," in *Evangelical Dictionary of Biblical Theology*, 451–454; Vos, *The Kingdom of God and the Church*, 21–23.

When we pray, "Thy kingdom come," are we praying for heaven to come to earth? In a sense we are praying for this; but heaven is an object of desire only because the reign of God is to be more perfectly realized than it is now. Apart from the reign of God, heaven is meaningless. Therefore, what we pray for is, "Thy kingdom come; *Thy will be done* on earth as it is in heaven." This prayer is a petition for God to reign, to manifest His kingly sovereignty and power, to put to flight every enemy of righteousness and of His divine rule, that God alone may be King over all the world.[4]

The doxology of the Lord's Prayer, though not included in many important ancient Greek manuscripts, further connects God's kingdom and authority in the disciples' minds. When they praised God for having the kingdom, power, and glory, they acknowledged that the same God who owns the kingdom has the power to rule it and the glory to attract people to it.[5]

In I Corinthians 15:25–28, Paul described the character of the kingdom of God precisely as Jesus did in the Lord's Prayer. The apostle declared concerning the Savior, "he must reign until he has put all his enemies under his feet. . . . When he has done this, then the Son himself will be made subject to him who put everything under him, so that God may be all in all."

The phrase "all in all" is comprehensive. It implies absolute rule over all things so that they radiate His glory. On the day He is "all in all," even the bells of the horses will tinkle to His praise (Zechariah 14:20). At that time all

---

4. Ladd, *The Gospel of the Kingdom*, 21.
5. Vos, *The Kingdom of God and the Church*, 51.

things great and small will fulfill their creative purpose and happily submit to the Lord's will.

At present, much of God's creation still opposes His rule (I John 5:19); but Scripture prophesies that this state of affairs is temporary (John 16:33; Luke 10:18–19; Romans 16:20; Hebrews 2:14). As we live in this world of sin, we must remember that earth's headlines are heaven's footnotes. The good news of heaven is that God's kingdom is on the march. The Lord has already begun to conquer His enemies and will soon destroy every opponent. Broadcast this news from your pulpit and your members will take note and take heart. In contrast, your daily newspapers will sound like doomsday! People want and need good news. You have it, and are called to deliver it!

The second characteristic of God's kingdom is its spirituality. Unlike kingdoms of this world, the divine kingdom is not formed by weapons, political and economic strategies, or coercion of the powers of state. Rather, God graciously establishes His kingdom by the internal renewal of hearts. Jesus, while explaining the uniqueness of His kingdom, said, "My kingdom is not of this world. If it were, my servants would fight to prevent my arrest by the Jews. But now my kingdom is from another place" (John 18:36).

Since the kingdom of God is spiritual, it does not consist of arrogant talk (I Corinthians 1:19–20) or eating and drinking, but of life-transforming power and joy in the Holy Spirit (Romans 14:17–18). As you emphasize the spirituality of God's kingdom, be careful that people do not conclude that it is ethereal, or limited to the soul and spirit. What Scripture means is that the kingdom's "center of activity," as someone has put it, is spiritual and internal; but this characteristic does not exclude physical manifestations.

Consider I Corinthians 15, where Paul contrasted "spiritual" with "natural," rather than with "physical." To be sown a natural body and raised a spiritual body means that the natural, sin-affected physical body will be raised a spiritual, sin-free physical body. Spiritual bodies are physical resurrected bodies that have been renewed by Christ and are controlled by the Spirit. If we deny the physical resurrection and thus also deny the physical character of heaven, we abandon faith. Either Christ died and arose to renew our entire person or His work was in vain.

That, most emphatically, is not the case! His atoning sacrifice is so effective and thorough that it not only will result in the redemption of believers' bodies and souls, but it will also rescue the entire world from the effects of sin. Christ's saving work, once begun, must continue until all of life and the whole creation is full of His glory (Romans 8:18–25).

Anthony Hoekema speaks in these expansive terms about the universal scope of the divine kingdom: "The kingdom must not be understood as merely the salvation of certain individuals or even as the reign of God in the hearts of His people; it means nothing less than the reign of God over His entire created universe."[6] Cornelius Plantinga Jr. likens our perspective of hope to a "wide-angle lens."[7] It not only "takes in whole nations and peoples" but also "brings into focus the entire created order—wolves and lambs, mountains and plains, rivers and valleys."[8] In another place Plantinga says, "The kingdom of God is the sphere of God's sovereignty—namely, the whole universe. In the vivid imagery of Isaiah 66:1, heaven is "God's throne" and the earth is "God's footstool." God is *God*, after all, the author

6. Hoekema, *The Bible and the Future*, 45.

7. Plantinga, *Engaging God's World: A Reformed Vision of Faith, Learning, and Living*, 13.

8. Ibid., 13–14.

of galaxies, the redeemer of all the earth, the "King of kings and Lord of lords."[9]

Because the kingdom is spiritual, its demands are spiritual. What does the divine kingdom demand? Simply put, it requires perfect righteousness. But how can God make such demands of us when we are incurably unrighteous? He does so only because God, Himself, provides, as a gift, the perfect righteousness that we need.

> The righteousness required for entrance into God's Kingdom is the righteousness which results from God's reign in our lives. The Kingdom of God gives to us that which it demands; otherwise, we could not attain to it. The righteousness which God requires is the righteousness of God's Kingdom which God imparts as He comes to rule within our lives.[10]

Since God's kingdom demands a righteousness that can be received only as a gift, the kingdom is *conferred upon* (Luke 22:29) or *given to* (12:32) those whom the Lord has called into it. If your preaching is to inspire hope, it must underscore the fact that the kingdom of God cannot be earned or achieved by human effort; rather, it is guaranteed to those who receive it in humble faith and repentance.

Preaching that God is creating a kingdom of righteousness with origins outside of this world gives hope. It does so despite the presence of human weakness and failure. Though we do not now think with absolute purity, there is coming a day when we will. And while we do not always speak in perfect love, we look forward to the day we will do so. Because the kingdom is coming, our eyes gaze heavenward in eager expectation. Perfect righteousness will prevail and we will see it with our own eyes (I John 3:2–3).

9. Plantinga, *Engaging God's World*, 107
10. Ladd, *The Gospel of the Kingdom*, 79.

With the glory of God's kingdom in view, our preaching will neither be dull nor prosaic. Rather, it will enliven, compel, and stimulate the saints. If love is a dominate characteristic of heaven then it should also mark the lives of believers on earth. And, if there is no mourning, crying, or pain in heaven then we should seek relief from misery and suffering on earth. (James 1:27). Believers, in Christ, begin to practice today on earth what they long for and will enjoy eternally in heaven. They don't suddenly become holy and heavenly minded just when they reach the gates of heaven! No, true believers' minds and hearts are being renewed right here and now as they wait for their Lord and Savior to return (Romans 12:1–2). Like leaven, the characteristics of the kingdom permeate and transform the lives of those who belong to it.

The Stages of the Kingdom

God's Word reveals that His kingly rule comes in progressive stages. It is important to distinguish three of them if you are to effectively preach the hope of the kingdom. They are Old Testament national Israel, this age, and the age to come.

Old Testament National Israel

God's kingdom rule in the Old Covenant was in the form of a theocracy. He ruled directly over His people by divinely given civil and ceremonial laws. Israel's kings were vice-regents under God. The purpose of the theocracy was that Israel would know, serve, and represent God before all the peoples of the earth and at the end of history enter, under His rule, into glory.

From its earliest history, Israel looked ahead in eschatological anticipation to a land flowing with milk and honey, freedom from all enemies, and the eternal administration of its own divinely appointed, internationally acclaimed ruler. Israel's hope was to enjoy God's favor and blessing forever.

The primary features that distinguished national Israel as a kingdom belonging to God are perhaps best summarized in Romans 9:4–5: "Theirs is the adoption as sons; theirs the divine glory, the covenants, the receiving of the law, the temple worship and the promises. Theirs are the patriarchs, and from them is traced the human ancestry of Christ." Israel knew God and revered Him as no people of the earth ever had. John Bright describes Israel's unique relationship with God in this way:

> Israel believed that her God both could and did control the events of history, that in them he might reveal his righteous judgment and saving power. Here is the sharpest break with paganism imaginable. The ancient pagans were all polytheistic, with dozens of gods arranged in complex pantheons. These gods were for the most part personifications of the forces of nature or other cosmic functions; they were in and of nature and, like nature, without any particular moral character. Their will could be manipulated in the ritual (which re-enacted the myth) so that they would bestow on the worshiper the desired tangible benefits. In such religions no moral interpretation of events, nor indeed any consistent interpretation, was possible, for no one god ruled history. The God of Israel is of a totally different sort. He controls sun, moon, and stars; works now in the fire, now in the storm—but he is identified with none of these. He has no fixed place of abode in heaven or on earth, but comes to the aid of his people and exhibits his power where he will, be it in Egypt, at Sinai, or in Canaan. He is no personification of natural force to be appeased by ritual (in

Israel's faith nature is "de-mythologize(d)"); he is a moral Being who controls nature and history, and in them reveals his righteous will and summons men to obey it.[11]

Israel not only knew God as a great and mighty Father, but also as Friend and Covenant-Partner. In response to God's invitation, Israel slipped its tiny hand into His to be escorted into its promised future land. Israel knew it was favored! Throughout its history, its status as God's bride shaped, for good or bad, everything it thought and did.

National Israel began as a small divinely-guided family. Under God's grace and protection it grew into a powerful God-centered kingdom. But, finally, it nearly disintegrated, under sovereign judgment, into a fragmented and humiliated remnant of its former glory. Despite the failures that marked its history, Israel's covenants, promises, and temple worship served as the foundation upon which its kingdom life was built. The Old Testament kingdom anticipated and foreshadowed another kingdom—one that would not pass away.

When we follow the path of kingdom history from the ancient past to our world today, we can see God's promises for the future fulfilled. God's pledge to Abraham that the patriarch would be the forefather of multinational progeny already became a reality in the Old Testament. But today it is even more dramatically fulfilled, as sons and daughters of faith from all over the world are adopted into God's royal, priestly family (Romans 4:16; Galatians 3:6–9; I Peter 2:9–10). Ultimately, the divine promise to Abraham will be fully realized in glory as the redeemed "from every tribe and language and people and nation" (Revelation 5:9) gather around the throne "to be a kingdom and priests to serve our God" (verse 10).

11. Bright, *The Kingdom of God*, 25–26.

Likewise, God's promise that Canaan will be an "everlasting possession" was initially fulfilled under Joshua. Today, it is being realized in a different way as sons and daughters of the "Israel of God" (Galatians 6:16) already yield their possessions and lives to His service. And in the future kingdom age, it will be perfectly experienced on the new earth as the saints reign over the whole divinely renewed and transformed creation (Revelation 20–21).

In summary, God guaranteed that He would establish His everlasting covenant. His pledge was reaffirmed through David and the prophets, fulfilled and made new through Christ's ministry and atoning blood sacrifice, and, in the end, will result in uninterrupted blessing in heaven.

The Kingdom in This Age

In the Old Testament, the kingdom reign of God appeared in its most rudimentary and sketchy form. This may seem strange since national Israel was a concrete entity and its commandments and rituals were very specific. But simply having definite boundaries, policies, and laws did not produce the spiritually mature kingdom that God desired. For that to happen, the Father's own Son had to come to live among His people and God's Spirit had to be poured out upon them.

When Jesus came, the kingdom took on such new and spiritually forceful dimensions that He spoke of it as just emerging (Matthew 4:17; Mark 1:14–15). In His own person, His "words and deeds, miracles and parables, teaching and preaching, the kingdom of God was dynamically active and present among men."[12] For the first time in human history, the kingdom of Satan suffered a crushing and permanent blow and the kingdom of God gained a decisive victory (John 12:31–32; Colossians 2:15). Jesus, having

12. Hoekema, *The Bible and the Future*, 43.

mastered storm, sin, demons, disease, and death, introduced the power of God's kingdom, demonstrated His absolute authority over every challenger, and bridled the activity of Satan (Hebrews 2:14–15).

Some in Christ's day expected the kingdom to appear as a divinely initiated human dictatorship.[13] So that no one would be mistaken by the divine kingdom's humble form, Jesus spoke in unambiguous terms about its arrival. His clearest words about the present reality of the kingdom were spoken in response to the Pharisees, who accused Christ of driving out demons by Beelzebub: "But if I drive out demons by the Spirit of God, then the kingdom of God *has come upon you*" (Matthew 12:28; emphasis mine).[14] Jesus reasoned that because Satan's power has been broken (see Hebrews 2:14), the kingdom has already begun. Furthermore, as God reduces Satan's power, He initiates His own rule and new order.

13. Lioy, *The Decalogue in the Sermon on the Mount*, 87. "In Jesus' day, the concept of the kingdom was rooted in the Old Testament. For instance, God's rule was eternal (Ps. 145:13) and universal (103:19), but it was only partially recognized on earth. In fact, all nations would not serve the Lord until the last days (Zech. 14:9). Jewish people prayed daily for the coming of God's reign. Also, when they prayed for His kingdom, they did not doubt that God presently reigned over His creation; yet they longed for the day when God would rule unchallenged and all peoples would acknowledge Him. Jesus' teachings about the kingdom show it was both present with Him on earth (Matt. 4:17) and also something that would be completely fulfilled at the end of the ages (13:24–30; 16:28). Jesus revealed that entrance into His kingdom is something that God gives to those who believe (25:34), but (paradoxically) it can cost a person everything he or she has (19:16–24)."

14. Note that in Matthew 12:28, the Greek verb *ephthasen* is in the aorist tense and means "has arrived" or "has come," not "is about to come." See the explanatory comments made on this verse in *The Net Bible*, Garland, Texas: Biblical Studies Press, L.L.C., and the authors, Web: http://www.bible.org/netbible/index.htm.

Another reference to the present reality of the kingdom of God is found in Luke 17:20–21. In this passage, Jesus' response to a question about when the kingdom would come indicates that He regarded it as having already arrived. He said, "The kingdom of God does not come with your careful observation, nor will people say, 'Here it is,' or 'There it is,' because the kingdom of God is within [or among] you."

By making this statement, Jesus was not denying that one day the Son of Man will be revealed in spectacular grandeur (Matthew 25:31); but He was making it clear that His second advent and the kingdom's initial arrival are not the same. The kingdom, indeed, has already come. It has done so quietly, internally, and often imperceptibly, but with radical impact. And the kingdom's arrival realigns allegiances and turns whatever it touches into an instrument of praise to God.

Of what importance is it that the kingdom has already come? It means that our Christian experience today relates directly to kingdom life in the world to come. It also means that our fear of death should be replaced with anticipation of glory.

How does preaching the presence of the kingdom of God tie Christian experience today to life in the age to come? Simply stated, it does so by showing that the same Lord and Spirit is at work in both ages. The Lord Jesus Christ, who is on the throne in heaven, is also the One who entered our world to rescue us from this "present evil age" (Galatians 1:4). He invaded the realm of the prince of the rulers of this world and the god of this age (John 12:30–33; Ephesians 2:1–3; 6:10–12) to break his stranglehold on the redeemed (Hebrews 2:14).[15] Having broken Satan's power

15. The phrase in the NIV translated "might destroy" has been variously paraphrased as "put [Satan] out of order," "render him inoperative," and "reduce to nothing."

and thrown him from the pinnacle of his might (Luke 10:18), Jesus ransacked his house (Matthew 12:29) and gave the devil's former subjects a foretaste of the powers of the age to come.

Because Jesus rescues believers from Satan, they long to live under the Savior's control. And because the redeemed are citizens of the kingdom of heaven (Ephesians 2:19; Philippians 3:20), more of Christ's rule means more freedom for them to enjoy the renewal that God's grace and power produce. It means a release from the tyranny of sin![16]

Power to live the holy life—the life of the age to come—is already a reality for us as Christians because the Spirit of our risen Lord now resides in us. We already have eternal life and already are raised from the dead in a provisional, spiritual form (John 17:3; Romans 6:4). The very life we will have for all eternity already pulsates within us. Even physical death does not interrupt it. For believers, the tomb purifies and perfects, and is a precursor of resurrection glory with the Triune God. This truth must be proclaimed. Where it is declared, the frost of despair melts and blossoms of hope peep into view!

How comforting and encouraging to know that the same Spirit who will fill and govern us perfectly in glory already lives within us. In fact, He is the down payment or

16. Release from the tyranny of sin is at the heart of Paul's argument in Romans 6. The apostle declared that, prior to trusting in Christ, the sinner was enslaved to the pull of sin. But the old self, having been crucified with Christ, is freed from this power. Sin no longer has any legal right to exercise its power in the life of the believer. The bondage has been broken. The controlling power is rendered inoperative. As Christians, we are often tempted to obey our old slave master. In fact, our sinful nature is like an old military commander who has been stripped of authority but still goes around barking orders, trying to get someone to obey. We are no longer slaves to this tyrant, but we must appropriate what God has provided. We must choose to live as free people.

earnest money of our future inheritance (Ephesians 1:13–14). Paul's figurative terms "firstfruits" (Romans 8:23) and "deposit" (Ephesians 1:14) imply that God will one day give us more of what we already have. The significance of the apostle's imagery is that the part represents the whole.[17]

As bales of wool in Paul's day were stamped with the purchaser's monogram when a down payment was made, so we were "sealed" with the Spirit when we were given His indwelling presence at the moment of our salvation. And, as the firstfruit of a crop is a sample of what will come, so we "have the firstfruits of the Spirit" and "groan inwardly as we wait eagerly for adoption as sons, the redemption of our bodies" (Romans 8:23). We know that life begun under the Spirit must necessarily end completely full of the Spirit. J. C. Beker describes the relationship between the present and the future work of the Spirit as follows:

> Thus, the Christ-event is not a closure—or a completed event. As "first fruits" it strains toward its actualization in the harvest of the final resurrection of the dead. . . . The necessary connection between Christ and the future triumph of God is confirmed by Paul's view of the Spirit. The Spirit is related to the future glory of God in the same manner that Christ is related to the future resurrection of the dead. In fact, the Spirit is the agent of the future glory in the present; it is the first down-payment or guarantee of the end-time (Romans 8:23; II Corinthians 1:22) and thus the signal of its coming.[18]

Understanding the continuity of the Spirit's activity in this age and the age to come naturally leads us to obedient and responsible Christian living. As those who are born

17. Gaffin, *The Centrality of the Resurrection*, 34–39.
18. Beker, *Paul's Apocalyptic Gospel*, 46.

of the Spirit, we must live the life of the Spirit (Galatians 5:25). It is incompatible to be born of the Spirit and despise the life of the Spirit. It is also utterly absurd and impossible to love God and live under His kingdom rule while at the same time loving sin (James 4:4; I John 2:15). To love sin means to deliberately choose sin and revel in its practice (Romans 1:32). This double mindedness cannot be maintained without eternally devastating consequences (Matthew 6:24; Hebrews 6:4–6).

When God's Spirit invades this age, a new creation appears. J. C. Beker noted the following: "Already the powers of the new age are at work in the church and already believers can resist the 'deeds of the body' (Romans 8:13) because of the presence of the Spirit—the sign of the new age—in their midst. Indeed, the Spirit enables 'a new creation' to occur in the midst of the old creation (II Corinthians 5:17)."[19]

Because we are new creations of the Spirit, God separates us from sin and orients us to live to His praise. Those appointed to salvation are also called to holiness and to God's kingdom and glory (I Thessalonians 2:12; 4:7; 5:9). Thus, to be saved is to be rescued from evil and the coming wrath and devoted to the true God, especially as we wait for His Son's return from heaven (I Thessalonians 1:9–10). Paul characterized the Christian life in one compact sentence. It is *serving* God as we *wait* for Jesus; and it is being made holy as we long for glory.

Responsible living "in Christ" fosters hope. There is hope in the fact that God Himself empowers us to live to His glory. There is also hope in performing simple, concrete acts of mercy in Jesus' name. These acts provide tangible evidence of kingdom life and are the very essence of God's rule in us (Matthew 5: 3–10; 43–47). It really is possible for us

19. Ibid., 40.

to begin to live the life of heaven right now in and through our daily activities. Heaven can touch earth in our presence, and our lives can begin to actually reflect the glory of God. Does your ethical preaching hold out this hope?

Preaching is revolutionary when it makes people aware that they can sample the life of eternity here and now. Not only does such preaching foster a surge of imaginative and dedicated ministry, but it also turns all of life into a quest for the glory of God (II Thessalonians 1:12; 2:14). This kind of preaching likewise creates an insatiable passion within us to shape every relationship, act, and moment after the pattern of the world to come.

I'm sure you know people who are motivated by this desire. It prompts them to willingly shoulder difficult tasks. Such individuals voluntarily do body-straining, mind-stretching ministries. They know the King reigns and is coming again to claim His kingdom.

If your perspective of Christian living and preaching doesn't reflect the continuity of hope between the present and coming stage of the kingdom, then your impetus for following Jesus is reduced to sheer, slug-it-out perseverance. Perseverance, rightly conceived, is not a bludgeoning of the will into stoic endurance of the intolerable. Rather, it is faithful, hope-inspired persistence while we are "being transformed into [Christ's] likeness with ever-increasing glory" (II Corinthians 3:18).

Preaching the Christian life as a foretaste of heaven delights and satisfies. It provides incredible joy, offers peace beyond understanding, and gives meaning to every breath of life. But such preaching does more than that. It replaces the fear of death with an anticipation of glory.

When dying saints meditate upon the fact that the same Redeemer who lives within them is also the Lord they are about to meet face to face, they are tremendously encouraged. Often the Messiah seems rather distant and remote when we think of Him as dying on the cross. But He becomes real and familiar when we regard Him as the One who currently lives within and renews us through His Spirit (John 14:15–21).

My father, who died of cancer in 1984, experienced this. During the final stages of his illness, his discomfort became intense, but it did not destroy his hope. Rather, he grew in hope! Why? It's because he knew that soon he would be in the presence of the very Lord who had already become his Ruler, Redeemer, and Friend. What hope! What a future!

Pastors who minister to hopeful, Spirit-controlled, dying believers know that often fear of death is almost totally replaced by eagerness for glory. Paul reflected this mindset in Philippians 1:21, "For to me, to live is Christ and to die is gain." Hopeful saints, who have their eyes fixed on things above during the course of life, find that Christ fills their vision when they die (Colossians 3:1-4).

Individual saints become strong in hope as they look heavenward. Likewise, whole churches and communities of believers can take aim on heaven, serve the King, and be transformed into centers of hope in our despairing world. They become so sure of what lies ahead that they set out to meet the future before it meets them.

The Kingdom in the Age to Come

The kingdom has come in reality, but it has not yet come in splendor. Therefore, we pray, wait, and hope. Sin and death constantly remind us that the perfect is still ahead. Thus, our prayer while we wait is, "Lord, come quickly!" (I Corinthians 16:22; Revelation 22:20).

Only Jesus' second coming can make the perfect appear. And what an event His Parousia will be! The Bible speaks of it in shocking, grand, and cosmic terms. There will be power, great glory, cataclysm, shaking, purging, melting, and renewal. When the King comes in power, His perfect kingdom will likewise appear in glory. Before Him all of earth's gates will lift their heads so that the King of glory may come in (Psalm 24:7–10).

When Jesus comes again and reveals His terrifying and awesome power, all sin and sorrow will be put away. Then, in a moment, He will bring into full view the perfect heavenly society and environment for which we long. Here is how Richard Mouw envisions the coming city of God.

> Isaiah 60 records a vision of [that] magnificent city. In it, the prophet is speaking *to* the city, calling attention to various aspects of its appearance. His tone is joyful, his mood excited. This city is not like any other that he has seen among the products of human efforts at urbanization; it is a city built by God. Sometimes Isaiah addresses the city in the present tense; at other points, he employs the language of future fulfillment. Though the city has not yet been established, he is certain that it will someday arrive. It is clearly a transformed city. Many of the people and objects from Isaiah's own day appear within its walls, but they have assumed different roles, they perform new functions.[20]

As Richard Mouw points out, culture will not be eliminated from the new earth, but its function will be changed. "Ships of Tarshish," rather than serving as symbols of pagan commercial power, will "become vessels for ministry in the transformed City." Lumber of Lebanon will "beautify the place of my sanctuary." And Midian's and Ephah's camels will "proclaim the praise of the Lord." What a glorious hope! Have you been preaching it?

20. Mouw, *When the Kings Come Marching In*, xii.

From the beginning of history God's people have yearned for shalom, that is, His perfect, unchanging, and eternal peace. Shalom reflects a setting in which the redeemed can be all God intended them to be, while at the same time enjoying the fullness of His blessing. Cornelius Plantinga Jr. observed that this is a "rich state of affairs in which natural needs are satisfied and natural gifts fully employed, all under the arch of God's love."[21] This "webbing together of God, humans, and all creation in justice, fulfillment, and delight"[22] will surely come to pass.

When the new heaven and new earth described in Scripture appear (Isaiah 11:6–9; 35; 60; Ezekiel 47:1–12; 48:30–35; Micah 4:1–4; Zechariah 14:6–21; Revelation 20–21), they will be composed of the transformed and sanctified materials of this world. Thus, our attempts to renew culture today relate immediately to our expectation of heaven and can, in anticipation of eternity, be offered as a hope-filled service of praise to God.

Preaching the Hope of the Kingdom

The concept of the kingdom is a major, sustained theme of hope throughout Scripture. From its beginning to its end, divine revelation points God's people forward to the day when the Lord will reign supreme as their eternal, glorious King. Therefore, if your church members are to grow strong in hope, it is imperative that you teach them about that kingdom and about the visionary future it presents.

Though Scripture often mentions the concept of the kingdom, you may find it a difficult subject to define and communicate. If you do, study it carefully, distill the full gambit of scriptural teaching on it, and then try to preach it

21. Plantinga, *Engaging God's World: A Reformed Vision of Faith, Learning, and Living*, 15.

22. Ibid., 14.

both directly and indirectly in relationship to other themes and passages of Scripture. Biblical hope remains weak until it is seen in the light of the kingdom of God. Because the teaching of the kingdom is complex, you will have to expound it again and again, and repeatedly identify the stage of the kingdom to which your preaching passage refers.

Our world is full of worry, tension and moral decay. We enjoy high technology but are often unable to use it for long-term benefit. Ulrich Fick, the former General Secretary of the United Bible Society, compared our civilization to "runners, running out of breath."

Believers know all too well that the kingdoms of this world are fractured, incomplete, and in disharmony. Peace agreements often fail. Dictators and governments topple. But Christ, the King of kings, has begun His transforming and eternal rule. Thus, as His church works to resolve problems and bring peace to homes, communities, and the world, it can do so in the serenity of hope.

If the theme of the kingdom threads its way throughout your messages, your congregation will develop an increasingly broad and solid foundation of hope upon which they can construct lives of Christian service. They will be able to see how their ministry of today relates to and is carried out in expectation of entering the "city with foundations, whose architect and builder is God" (Hebrews 11:10).

Faithful preaching of hope demands that we point people forward to the full revelation of God's kingdom, the New Jerusalem. Be sure to preach it. When you do you will be helping your congregants to stand strong through the struggles of life.

CHAPTER SIX

Preaching the Hope of the Presence of God

WITH PROPER decorum, the wedding party took its
position at the marriage altar. After opening his black
wedding manual, the minister began to read, "Here in the
presence of God . . ." Then he paused for rhe-
torical effect. The young ring-bearer, unaware
of the purpose of such a pause and momentarily
oblivious to his surroundings, locked on the
word presence. Suddenly his thoughts tumbled
out in loud, crisp words, "Presents, presents,
who's got presents?"

As you can imagine, the whole solemn as-
sembly erupted into laughter. How funny! How
incongruous! But there may have been another
incongruity that no one noticed. Could it be that many of
the laughing guests themselves were no more aware of what
it meant to be in the presence of God than the ring-bearer?

Based on my analysis of about 200 sermons and on
conversations with members of my own and other congregations, I've found that the subject of the presence of
God receives very little attention in pulpits today. It's little
wonder that few people understand its meaning, reality, and
importance.

So what is "the presence of God"? It refers to something
more specific than God's omnipresence.[1] It is a discernable

1. The theological term "omnipresence" refers to the divine
characteristic of being ever present in all places at all times. Although
God is simultaneously and instantaneously present everywhere in
His creation, He is not limited by it in any way (see 1 Kings 8:27;

nearness to God's person. The presence of God connotes the face of God[2] and implies the concentration of His majesty, might, and glory. To be in God's presence is to be close enough to the Lord to see Him as He is and transparent enough to invite Him to see us as we are.[3]

When you come before God's face, you discern Him with enough clarity to read His expression. Faces reveal emotion. They may be cheerful, brilliant, shining, sad, or angry. As Psalm 34:15–16 indicates, God's face shows both welcome and threat: "The eyes of the LORD are on the righteous, and his ears are attentive to their cry; the face of the LORD is against those who do evil, to cut off the memory of them from the earth."

The opposite of "face" is "back." To thrust God behind our backs (Ezekiel 23:35) is to reject and forget the Lord. Similarly, when God shows people His back (Jeremiah 18:17), they are doomed to judgment, wrath, and disaster.

God's face conveys approval and protection to those who revere Him. Having God's face shine upon us im-

II Chronicles 2:6; Psalm 139:7–12; Isaiah 66:1; Jeremiah 23:23–24).

2. In the Old Testament, *presence* almost always relates to "face" (Genesis 3:8; Exodus 33:14–23; Psalm 95:2; Isaiah 63:9). And occasionally *presence* refers to "eye" (Genesis 23:11; Deuteronomy 25:9; Jeremiah 28:1, 11). Of course, both *face* and *eye* are used in these contexts as anthropomorphisms (that is, the attributing of human forms or traits to the divine). The terms do not imply that God actually has a material or visible face. See Opperwall, "Presence," in *The International Standard Bible Encyclopedia,* 3:955.

3. It is true that God not only "lives in unapproachable light" (1 Tim. 6:16), but also that no one can see Him or ever truly see Him in the fullness of His heavenly splendor and glory. This fact notwithstanding, there is a sense in which, when the Savior returns, we will see Him as He really is (1 John 3:2). Indeed, the Christian hope is that God will one day be with His people and they will be with Him (Revelation 21:3). See Harrison, "Presence of God," in *The International Standard Bible Encyclopedia*, 3:956–957.

plies experiencing His safety and security. It makes us feel like the vacationing two-year-old who snuggled near her mother in an unfamiliar guest bed. When her mother rolled away, the child tugged on her mother's arm and said in her most pleading voice, "Mommy, put your face by me." The mother's face—even though her eyes were shut in sleep—communicated comfort and protection; but her back conveyed loneliness and fear.

Saints long to see God's face. They want to be near His gracious, sovereign person, look with fixed gaze on His majesty, admire His glory, and be wrapped in the secure confidence of His embrace (Psalm 27:4). Their greatest joy is to have the Lord's face shine upon them as they worship, love, and adore Him (Numbers 6:24–26).

If your preaching doesn't reveal God's face, it lacks an essential factor in communicating hope and in defining the goal towards which believing hope must move. It is impossible to inspire people to be attracted to a vague, faceless God, and love an expressionless Deity.

Hopeful believers crave the revealed face of God. Their hearts are drawn irresistibly to the brilliance of His glory (Psalm 27:8). They yearn to be with the Lord and live in His house (Psalm 23:6).

Heaven[4] has many attractions, such as unimpaired splendor, life without pain, and relationships without sin. All of these, however, are empty apart from God's presence. Heaven is peace and joy before God's unveiled face! It is living in perfect security in the presence of the Almighty.

Dying believers often become the most eager students of the hope of heaven. They are keenly aware that within moments they will step from this life into the very presence

---

4. In Scripture, "heaven" is often used to refer to the dwelling place of God as well as the eternal location for God's people in eternity (Deuteronomy. 26:15; Matthew 5:45). See Schoonhoven, "Heaven," in *The International Standard Bible Encyclopedia*, 2:654–655.

of God. As life fades and that which is temporary loses its alure, their minds strain ahead to their meeting with the Lord. What will He be like? How glorious is He? What will He say? If you help them discover God's answers to their urgent questions, you will be like an angel of hope.

Although the dying are usually the most receptive to preaching about heaven, all believers must prepare themselves to meet God. True Christians hunger for unobstructed fellowship with Him. They feel the longing voiced by the sons of Korah recorded in Psalm 42:1–2, "As the deer pants for streams of water, so my soul pants for you, O God. My soul thirsts for God, for the living God. Where can I go to meet with God?"

How important is it to meet with the Lord—to be in intimate communion with Him and know Him as He really is? It is an all-consuming passion! It is the goal and quest of new life in Christ.

The Glory of God's Presence

Scripture depicts God as being awesome and magnificent; therefore, His presence stuns and humbles all who enter it. One of the clearest examples of the staggering glory of the Lord's presence is found in Isaiah 6. Suddenly, the sovereign One appeared,[5] enthroned in His heavenly palace. His robe was so great and splendid that it filled His entire temple! Seraphic attendants sang God's glory: "Holy, holy, holy is the LORD Almighty; the whole earth is full of his glory"

5. In John 12:41, we read that Isaiah "saw Jesus' glory." The *Net Bible* offers this helpful explanation: "It is clear that the author presents Isaiah as having seen the preincarnate glory of Christ, which was the very revelation of the Father (see John 1:18; John 14:9). . . . On the basis of statements like 1:14 in the prologue, the author probably put no great distinction between the two. Since for the author Jesus is fully God, it presents no problem to him to take words originally spoken by Isaiah of Yahweh himself and apply them to Jesus."

(Isaiah 6:3). The divine is thrice holy and three times exalted! Isaiah could not miss it. Everything in sight recognized it. Even the doorposts and thresholds of the heavenly sanctuary shook and trembled in reverent awe.[6]

Meeting God is not like meeting people. Human encounters sometimes cause nervousness, worry, or uneasiness. But meeting God causes trembling. Before Him, we are exposed, naked, sinful, weak, and dependent. In His presence we see ourselves as we really are. R. C. Sproul offers these clarifying thoughts: "When we are aware of the presence of God, we become most aware of ourselves as creatures. When we meet the Absolute, we know immediately that we are not absolute. When we meet the Infinite, we become acutely conscious that we are finite. When we meet the Eternal, we know we are temporal. To meet God is a powerful study in contrasts."[7]

When Isaiah saw God, the prophet did what all who see God must do. Isaiah acknowledged his sin and repented (Isaiah 6:1–7; see also Job 42:5–6; Psalms 11:7; Psalm 51; Matthew 5:8). We are often led to believe that the first response to meeting God is joy, peace, comfort, or hope. But that is not so. Real encounters with the Lord begin with repentance and then produce other delightful emotions (Psalms 16:11; 21:6; 51:10 –17; 100:1–2).

Isaiah's encounter with God left the prophet feeling shaken as well as ruined and undone. R. C. Sproul paints the scene of Isaiah's experience with such vividness that we can almost see the prophet's body tremble:

---

6. Scripture often portrays inanimate creation responding strongly to the glory of God's presence. For example, it trembles before Him and yields to His desires (see Psalms 114; 119:120; Isaiah 64:1–3; Ezekiel 38:20; Nahum 1:3–6).

7. Sproul, *The Holiness of God*, 41.

To be undone means to come apart at the seams, to be unraveled. What Isaiah was expressing is what modern psychologists describe as the experience of personal disintegration. To disintegrate means exactly what the word suggests— *dis integrate*. If ever there was a man of integrity, it was Isaiah Ben Amoz. He was a whole man, a together-type of fellow. He was considered by his contemporaries as the most righteous man in the nation. He was respected as a paragon of virtue. Then, he caught one sudden glimpse of a holy God. In that single moment, all of his self-esteem was shattered. In a brief second, he was exposed, made naked beneath the gaze of the absolute standard of holiness. As long as Isaiah could compare himself to other mortals, he was able to sustain a lofty opinion of his own character. The instant he measured himself by the ultimate standard, he was destroyed—morally and spiritually annihilated. He was undone. He came apart. His sense of integrity collapsed.[8]

Trembling and awe are appropriate responses to God's glory. When the ark of the covenant entered Jerusalem, David, the leader and king of God's people, declared that the whole earth should tremble before the splendor of the Lord's holiness (I Chronicles 16:27–30). God's unmistakable providential care impelled Jeremiah to demand that unfaithful Israel develop a renewed and proper respect for the Lord's majestic greatness: "'Should you not fear Me?' declares the LORD. 'Should you not tremble in my presence? I made the sand a boundary for the sea, an everlasting barrier it cannot cross. The waves may roll, but they cannot prevail; they may roar, but they cannot cross it'" (Jeremiah 5:22).

8. Ibid., 43–44.

During the earliest days of redemptive history, God revealed Himself by rebuking the sea and causing mountains to quake. Even Gentiles, who were recipients of no special revelation, should have learned to humble themselves before the Lord's awesome power. Rahab did and was saved (James 2:25). Nineveh, on the other hand, refused to tremble at God's presence; consequently, the city and its inhabitants reeled before His indignation and fierce wrath (Nahum 1:5–6).

Modern society, with its secular attitudes, seems to have no stronger sense of the majestic presence of God than did ancient Nineveh. Ethical decisions, political choices, educational curricula, and social patterns are frequently established without regard to God. The masses, being governed by the people, the majority of whom no longer know God, flounder, morally adrift.

Likewise the church, being influenced by its surroundings, is often unaware of or unimpressed by God's glory. Instead of leading culture to Christ, the church often follows it away from Christ. J. I. Packer, while commenting on this lack of sensitivity to the majesty of God, notes the following:

> This is knowledge, which Christians today largely lack: and that is one reason why our faith is so feeble and our worship so flabby. We are modern men, and modern men, though they cherish great thoughts of man, have as a rule small thoughts of God. When the man in the street uses the word "God", the thought in his mind is rarely of divine *majesty*. . . . We are poles apart from our evangelical forefathers at this point, even when we confess our faith in their words. When you start reading Luther, or Edwards, or Whitefield, though your doctrine may be theirs, you soon find yourself wonder-

> ing whether you have any acquaintance at all with the mighty God whom they knew so intimately.[9]

Because our God has become so tiny and unimpressive, our hope has correspondingly diminished. Observing this phenomenon, Roger C. Palms offers this astute explanation:

> When we treat God casually, when we have a buddy-buddy, arm-around-the-shoulder, Jesus-as-best-friend relationship and lose the wonder of who God is, we also lose hope. Wonder and hope are intertwined. Why? Because wonder causes us to be in awe, to bow the head, to drop to our knees, to express our limits that grasps our souls, the more reason we have for hope.[10]

True knowledge of God bends our knees. As we bow in awe before Him, we feel something strange and wonderful. We sense that the very power and glory of God that caused us to tremble has become our protective shield (Genesis 15:1; Psalms 27:4–6; 44:3; 46; 73:27–28; 145:18–20; Zechariah 2:5). In love and mercy, the Lord spreads His wings over us and forgives us (Psalms 43; 61).

What a privilege it is for believers to see God's glory without being consumed by it! What an honor it is to be near enough to His majesty to exult in it! What a blessing it is to worship the Lord in the splendor of His holiness! Astounding as it may be, this is the believer's unique prerogative both here and now, and in the life to come.

9. Packer, *Knowing God*, 73–74.
10. Palms, *Bible Readings on Hope*, 102.

The Goal of Biblical Hope

In chapter two, we saw that the *focus* of biblical hope is the return of Jesus and the resurrection of the dead. But what is the *goal* of biblical hope? According to Scripture, history begins and ends with humankind living in the immediate presence of God. Therefore, the goal of life is unmistakable. It is to be near God and enjoy uninhibited fellowship with Him.

What a lofty goal! But is it attainable in this life? The answer is yes, in its provisional form. We who know the hope of the gospel and have experienced the indwelling of God's Spirit have already begun to enjoy the communion with God that will be ours through all eternity. When you hold this fact before your congregation, they will be spurred on by what they already know and possess, rather than reined in and defeated by remaining imperfections.

The poets of Israel's past clearly understood the powerful attraction of perfect life in God's presence. Consider the following verses from the Book of Psalms: "One thing I ask of the LORD, this is what I seek: that I may dwell in the house of the LORD all the days of my life, to gaze upon the beauty of the LORD and to seek him in his temple" (27:4). "But as for me, it is good to be near God. I have made the Sovereign LORD my refuge" (73:28). "How lovely is your dwelling place, O LORD Almighty! My soul yearns, even faints for the courts of the LORD; my heart and my flesh cry out for the living God" (84:1–2).

Failure to Meet the Goal of Hope

Though nearness to God is sublime and enticing, it is not the goal of most people. Rather than being drawn to the Lord, many feel repelled by Him and fear His presence.[11]

11. See chapter seven for survey data on this subject.

Redemptive history, which is the record of God's saving work between the perfection of Eden and the New Jerusalem, leaves no doubt as to why people feel this way.

Pre-fall Eden was distinct from the rest of human history. It was perfect. There, man listened to God and did His will, and God met his needs. In the cool of the evening, God manifested His presence in the garden and talked with Adam.

Then, when sin entered, fellowship with God was broken and man was expelled from Paradise. From that moment on, every human heart has sensed an inner conflict. It feels the urge to hide from God for fear of exposure, but it also senses the need to seek God for His protection.

Cain verbalized this dilemma when God confronted him with his sin: "Today you are driving me from the land," Cain protested. "And I will be hidden from your presence; I will be a restless wanderer on the earth, and whoever finds me will kill me" (Genesis 4:14).

Wandering and leisurely drifting might sound like fun in a folk ballad, but the restless roving of a homeless, hunted fugitive is misery. This roaming is burdensome and tiring. It is this kind of frightening and purposeless peregrination that the preaching of intimacy with God is intended to relieve.

To give His people security and hope, God Himself became their ever-present joy, reward, shield, and defense. For instance, during the exodus pilgrimage, He visibly accompanied His people. His abiding presence made them unique from all the other people of the earth (Exodus 40:36–38; Deuteronomy 7:6).

Without God's presence, Israel would have been like the pagans. Moses, while reflecting on what made Israel distinctive, made the following plea to the Lord: "If your Presence does not go with us, do not send us up from here. How will anyone know that you are pleased with me and with your people unless you go with us? What else will distinguish me and your people from all other people on the face of the earth?" (Exodus 33:15–16).

Though the Israelites knew that they were to live and move with God, they gradually disregarded their distinctiveness, and turned their backs on Him (Jeremiah 2:27; Malachi 1:6). So God, in faithfulness to His own Word and covenant (Deuteronomy 30:17–18), had to act contrary to the yearning of His fatherly heart and abandon His children to the loneliness their behavior deserved (Jeremiah 3:19; 31:9).

Alone and vulnerable, the Israelites cried out to God, "O Hope of Israel, its Savior in times of distress, why are you like a stranger in the land, like a traveler who stays only a night? Why are you like a man taken by surprise, like a warrior powerless to save? You are among us, O LORD, and we bear your name; do not forsake us!" (Jeremiah 14:8–9).[12]

Because the people's repentance was temporary and their remorse insincere, God's mercy to Israel had to be interrupted by punishment. But Ezekiel, while preaching God's message of hope, predicted a day in the future when the Lord would forever reside with them in grace.

> My servant David will be king over them, and they will all have one shepherd. They will follow my laws and be careful to keep my decrees. They will live in the land I gave to my servant Jacob, the land where your fathers lived. They and their children and their children's children will live there forever, and David my servant will be their prince forever. I will make a covenant of peace with them; it will be an everlasting covenant. I will establish them and increase

12. See also Isaiah 8:18; 30:27–29; 31:9; Jeremiah 7:12–15; 8:19; 23:23, 39; Ezekiel 8:6; Hosea 5:15; 11:9; Amos 1:2; 5:14; Micah 1:2–3; 3:11; 6:6.

> their numbers, and I will put my sanctuary among them forever. My dwelling place will be with them; I will be their God, and they will be my people. Then the nations will know that I the LORD make Israel holy, when my sanctuary is among them forever. (Ezekiel 37:24–28; see also 43:9)

From these verses we see that Ezekiel preached the most amazing and profound hope the world has ever known, namely, the hope of living with God forever. Likewise Zephaniah, in his preaching, held out the great hope of enjoying God's abiding presence:

> The Lord has taken away your punishment, he has turned back your enemy. The Lord, the King of Israel, is with you; never again will you fear any harm. On that day they will say to Jerusalem, "Do not fear, O Zion; do not let your hands hang limp. The Lord your God is with you, he is mighty to save. He will take great delight in you, he will quiet you with his love, he will rejoice over you with singing." (Zephaniah 3:15–17)

A Time of Fresh Hope

The time foretold by Ezekiel, Zephaniah, and other Old Testament preachers of hope has arrived! The day of God's permanent presence has come. At Jesus' incarnation, He tabernacled[13] among us (John 1:14); and following His

---

13. According to the *Net Bible*, the Greek word rendered "made his dwelling" (John 1:14) "alludes to the [Old Testament] tabernacle, where the Shekinah, the visible glory of God's presence, resided. The author is suggesting that this glory can now be seen in Jesus. . . . The verb used here may imply that the Shekinah glory that used to be found in the tabernacle has taken up residence in the person of Jesus" (see also 2:19–21).

return to heaven, His Spirit has come to stay. (John 16:7; Acts 2:1–4)

Since believers already have begun to experience the initial fulfillment of the promise of God's abiding presence, we look forward in eager hope to the event that will bring about the full realization of that promise, the Parousia.[14] Then, seeing Jesus as He truly is (I John 3:2), we will be united with Him forever in His perfecting presence (I Thessalonians 4:13–18). John described the coming of that new, eternal order of things in these words:

> I saw the Holy City, the new Jerusalem, coming down out of heaven from God, prepared as a bride beautifully dressed for her husband. And I heard a loud voice from the throne saying, "Now the dwelling of God is with men, and he will live with them. They will be his people, and God himself will be with them and be their God. He will wipe every tear from their eyes. There will be no more death or mourning or crying or pain, for the old order of things has passed away." (Revelation 21:2–4)

How exhilarating to preach this hope! It is the most exalted hope possible to humankind, and it is a hope that is sure to be satisfied. What is that hope? It is to live forever in God's majestic presence.

---

14. In its fundamental meaning, *parousia* indicates presence, that is, being near, by, or with some entity. Thus, for example, in Philippians 2:12, Paul contrasted his presence (or *parousia*) with his absence (*apousia*). When *parousia* refers to Jesus' return from heaven, it usually stresses the arrival or coming of His presence rather than His continuing presence (see James 5:7–8; 2 Peter 3:4). In either case, *parousia* always retains the idea of "presence" as part of its essential meaning. See Morris, "Parousia," in *The International Standard Bible Encyclopedia*, 3:664.

The Symbols of God's Presence

Biblical history reveals the goal of hope and so do biblical symbols. Though usually silent, their visual testimonies forcefully declare that God wants us to meet Him in glory.

Altars (places of sacrifice) were the earliest symbols used by the God-fearing. At first, they were simply rough, improvised heaps of unhewn stones. Crude as they were, they provided a place where God would come to His people and bless them (Exodus 20:24–26). They silently announced His welcome. "Come and meet Me," they said on behalf of God. "I invite you in grace" (see Genesis 28:18–19).

When the tabernacle was built, two specifically designed altars were constructed. One was an altar of burnt offering for thanksgiving and expiation, and the second was an altar of incense for the acknowledgement of God and for prayer. The Lord commanded that the altar of incense should stand in front of the curtain, before the ark of the testimony, where He would meet His people (Exodus 30:6).

Since altars symbolized meeting with God, they were anointed with oil. When this procedure was performed, one symbol of God's presence was sanctified by another. Oil was used to consecrate both objects that fulfill a sacred purpose and people who occupy a holy office.

The ark of the testimony (or covenant), more than all other symbols, conveyed the idea of meeting God in His mercy. This traveling sanctuary of God's presence had a lid (or mercy seat) adorned with two facing cherubs. "There," God said to Moses, "above the cover between the two cherubim that are over the ark of the Testimony, I will meet with you and give you all my commands for the Israelites" (Exodus 25:22).

Another visible symbol of God's presence was the cloud that accompanied the tribes during the Exodus. As

God met His people at Mount Sinai, the cloud of His presence was thick, dark, and fiery. It was dangerous and verbal, for God was in it.

Though the cloud of God's holy presence threatened, it also comforted. For Israel, it served as a cloud of protection. It was their guide and shield in battle (Exodus 13:20–22; 14:19–20). Wherever the Shekinah cloud appeared, whether on the mountain, as a sojourn guide, or at the sanctuary of meeting, it reminded the covenant people that God Himself was with them. The Lord was near to receive their honor and praise as their refuge and strength!

Because the symbols God gave Israel were sacred emblems of His presence, it is heartrending to read of their desecration, deportation, and destruction. One of the most tragic moments in Israel's history was when the temple, the house of God's dwelling, was dismantled and its treasures removed. How unimaginable that even the kings of Judah, whose task it was to fight Israel's battles and preserve God's people for the Lord, should turn from Him and barter away the symbol of His presence.

Ahaz was one such king. As he cowered in fear before Tiglath-Pileser, the king of Assyria, Ahaz gave this pagan monarch the temple's silver and gold. Furthermore, he dismantled the original temple altar. Then, in deference to Assyria's king, Ahaz built a Damascus-designed altar in its place (II Kings 16). This was rejection of God at its blatant worst!

Sadly, denuding the temple of its furnishings did not satisfy the God-despising motives of Manasseh, a subsequent king of Judah. (He was the son of Hezekiah and the grandson of Ahaz.) Manasseh's efforts to demean, dishonor, and ridicule the name of God knew no bounds. In arrogant disrespect of the Lord, Manasseh rebuilt the high places Hezekiah had torn down (II Kings 18:1–4), erected altars to Baal,[15] made an Asherah[16] pole, and bowed down to and built altars for all the starry hosts in the temple court, the same place God said He would put His Name. Manasseh also practiced sorcery and divination, consulted mediums and spiritists, and even sacrificed his own son in the fire (II Kings 21:1–18).

Since Judah thoroughly and deliberately rejected the Lord, at long last God determined, in accordance with His covenant promise, "to remove them from his presence" (II Kings 24:3). Not even the godly reign of Josiah (the son of Amon and grandson of Manasseh) could forestall divine judgment (II Kings 23:26–27). The Lord no longer was willing to tolerate the sinful ways of His people!

Evidences of God's decision were seen in what He allowed to happen to His temple. A wicked Judean king named Zedekiah "rebelled against the king of Babylon" (II Kings 24:20). This monarch was Nebuchadnezzar. In 588 B.C., he besieged Jerusalem. But it was not until 586 B.C. that the city finally fell (II Kings 25:1–7). After the Babylonian army removed all the treasures of the temple of the Lord and all the gold articles that Solomon, a former king of Israel, had made for it, the invaders set fire to the sanctuary and burned it down (verses 8–15).

Why had the Lord, the glory of Israel, departed? It was because God's people had spurned His presence! What a warning the account of these events is to preachers of hope. God's people can easily forget where they are headed. The preached Word must keep them looking at the face of God.

15. Baal was the supreme fertility and nature god of the Canaanites.

16. Asherah was a Canaanite fertility goddess, the wife of Asir (the god of war), and the mother of Baal. The word *asherah* also refers to a wooden pole (such as the trunk of a tree with the branches removed) where pagan sexual rites were performed.

With Israel's demise and the birth of the New Testament church, the use of Old Testament symbols of God's presence stopped.[17] But the goal for which they were intended and the reality to which they pointed did not end. According to the author of Hebrews, Jesus, our eternally installed High Priest, "entered heaven itself, now to appear for us in God's presence" (Hebrews 9:24). There the Messiah serves in the *true* tabernacle (Hebrews 8:1–6), which is neither man-made nor part of this creation (Hebrews 9:11).

One way our heavenly High Priest serves us today is by meeting us, through His Spirit, in the New Covenant sacraments of baptism and the Lord's Supper. As was the case during the Old Covenant, symbols seal our ongoing relationship with Yahweh. God Himself is present with us in grace guaranteeing, with visible promises, the reliability of His redeeming Word. In the sacraments God turns us in three directions—He takes us back to the cross, He applies the grace of the cross to our hearts today, and He lifts our heads to anticipate the wedding feast of the Lamb in the future.

Since Jesus is in heaven for us before the face of God, how much hope of entering God's presence can we have? Our hope can and should be absolute and without doubt. Do you have it? Do the members of your church? If not, meditate on where Christ is and take heart. Then preach this message of hope to your congregation. When you do, they'll lift their heads high with confident anticipation.

17. Admittedly, some later Old Testament prophets (for example, Ezekiel and Zechariah) speak of future sacrifice being offered, but their words have an historical and figurative dimension. Their pronouncements must refer literally to the Second Temple and figuratively to the perfect, holy sanctuary of the New Jerusalem; otherwise, the author of Hebrews would contradict what is revealed in the sacred Old Testament writings.

Preaching the Hope of God's Presence

Based on my previous analysis of hundreds of sermons, it's clear that the concept of the presence of God is sorely neglected in pulpits today. Contemporary religious literature also slights it. As a result, very few Christians give much thought to the meaning and importance of God's presence. This must be changed, especially if the experience and reality of life before God's face is to become the profound hope for His people that God intends it to be.

How should the hope of entering God's presence be preached? The answer to this question is at least twofold. First, the subject of entering God's presence should assume the same prominence in our preaching that it has in the Bible. To properly communicate the hope of God's presence, preachers themselves need to see and appreciate this concept in Scripture. Preachers who watch for references to God's presence as they read, meditate on, study, and analyze His Word, will naturally increase their references to it from the pulpit.

Second, to faithfully preach the hope of the presence of God, some pastors will have to increase their number of "now that" sermons. Read the advertised topics of Sunday messages in your local newspaper. You will probably discover that there is much "how to" mania among preachers in your community. Many sermons today are like fix-it manuals. They give the solutions to repairing everything from depression, to child behavior, to attitudes, to sex. They center on the wishes, feelings, aspirations, desires, and praise of people. But these sermons fail to point out that we are living before the face of God, and that everything we say and do must glorify and honor Him.

Sermons that aim to teach people how to function or behave have some value, but they are often of minimal consequence in preparing people to meet God. Growth in the hope of beholding God's face requires a regular diet of sermons that show people who God is and what He has done. "How to" sermons may fill pews, but "now that" sermons fill hearts.

What is a "now that" sermon? In "now that" sermons you hear phrases like, "Now that God is who He is . . ." and, "now that God has acted as He has . . ." It is a sermon that accentuates the character and actions of God. A "now that" sermon invites people to see God in His glory. Effective "now that" sermons provide the basis for proper "how to" applications. "How to" sermons put prescriptions in people's hands, but give them no good reasons to have them filled.

If we want to encourage people in the thoroughly biblical hope of entering the presence of God, we need preaching that sounds more like that of the pulpit giants of years gone by.[18] Preaching should not be "stuffy" or unrelated to life; but should direct people to the already complete, ongoing, and future work of Christ.

Preaching that disregards the firm foundation of hope proclaimed in Scripture, holds people captive to small expectations. But preaching that accurately expounds the Bible's hope, liberates believers to expect the blessings in store for those upon whom God's face shines and His favor rests.

When sermons reflect God's majesty and divinity, they have the power to encourage and console. Think, for

18. For example, consider these sermon titles of John Flavel, an early Puritan preacher of England, who proclaimed and wrote the following "under the pressure of persecution and possible arrest": Union with Christ; Christ Applied to Believers; the Work of the Spirit; Fellowship with Christ; Christ, the Physician of Souls; Christ, the Merciful; Christ, the Desire of Nations; and Acceptance with God. These titles are taken from *The Method of Grace: How the Holy Spirit Works*.

example, of the impact of the following words from Psalm 77 on a person facing terminal illness or abuse of a spouse, if they are lovingly and accurately communicated by their pastor.

> I cried out to God for help; I cried out to God to hear me. When I was in distress, I sought the Lord; at night I stretched out untiring hands and my soul refused to be comforted. . . . Will the Lord reject us forever? Will he never show his favor again? . . . Then I thought, "To this I will appeal: the years of the right hand of the Most High." I will remember the deeds of the LORD; yes, I will remember your miracles of long ago. I will meditate on all your works and consider all your mighty deeds. Your ways, O God, are holy. What god is so great as our God? You are the God who performs miracles; you display your power among the peoples. With your mighty arm you redeemed your people, the descendents of Jacob and Joseph. (Psalm 77:1–2, 7, 10–15)

When hope and comfort are needed to pass through the valleys of life, they will be found by meeting with God in person. Preachers of God's hope, invite your listeners to see the Lord today and prepare them to meet Him face-to-face tomorrow!

CHAPTER SEVEN

Preaching the Hope of the Judgment

IF THE red-faced, glowering caricature of preachers in movies[1] has influenced your attitude regarding preaching God's judgment, you likely envision the judgment as negative, oppressive, threatening, onerous, harsh, cold, unfair, and condemnatory. It's hardly a subject you would choose for a message of hope!

If, however, Moses, Peter, and Paul have shaped your opinion about preaching judgment, you might very well pick that topic as your theme of hope. Scripture reveals that the judgment purifies the world of evil, pain, suffering, and disease, vindicates the holiness of God, halts the enemies of Christ and His church, and opens the door to the new heaven and earth, the home of righteousness. For true, born-again believers, the judgment is *good* news. It's a fountainhead of encouragement and a stimulant to godliness, not a source of despair or terror (II Peter 3:11–14).

If the judgment is desirable to those who hate sin and want it purged, it necessarily sounds frightening to anyone practicing evil (I Peter 4:17–18). In judgment, sin-lovers are the enemy and almighty God is the attacker! How dreadful it is to fall into the hands of an angry God![2]

1. For example, John Lithgow in *Footloose* (Hollywood, California: Paramount Home Video, 1984).

2. Hebrews 10:31 is the foundation for this statement: "It is a dreadful thing to fall into the hands of the living God." And in 12:29

Indeed, the judgment is *bad* news for everyone living apart from Christ. But even for them, preaching the judgment is potentially good news, especially if they are told that Christ is the one and only way of escape. Jonathan Edwards' famous sermon, "Sinners in the Hands of an Angry God," was welcome news for believers, but for those without Christ, Edwards' message was hard-hitting and direct:

> O sinner! Consider the fearful danger you are in: it is a great furnace of wrath, a wide and bottomless pit, full of the fire of wrath, that you are held over in the hand of that God, whose wrath is provoked and incensed as much against you as many of the damned in hell. You hang by a slender thread, with the flames of divine wrath flashing about it, and ready every moment to singe it and burn it asunder; and you have no interest in any Mediator, and nothing to lay hold of to save yourself, nothing to keep off the flames of wrath, nothing of your own, nothing that you have ever done, nothing that you can do to induce God to spare you one moment.[3]

Edwards' words pierced and convicted, but believing hearers went home confident of the greatness of God's mercy in Christ, not fearful and unsure of whether they had met God's requirements. As the *Annals of America* explains, Edwards "coil[ed] a monstrous accusation against mankind," and "bent the bow of God's wrath" with its arrow "aimed at the entrails of the race," but he never released it. Indeed, Edwards' message is a masterpiece of creating hope through the proclamation of judgment. It is not "an instance of Puritan delight in visions of hellfire." With the

we find the rationale: "for our 'God is a consuming fire.'"

3. Edwards, "Sinners in the Hands of an Angry God," in *Annals of America*, 423ff.

proper emphasis on God's grace, judgment can be preached hopefully.

Whatever Happened to Hell?

Because the final judgment is too distasteful and dogmatic for many modern spiritual palates, present-day preachers seldom mention it. B. A. Milne notes this conspicuous omission in his entry on the judgment in *The Illustrated Bible Dictionary:*

> There are few points at which the teaching in the Bible is more sharply in contrast with the assumptions of our age than in its teaching concerning God's judgment of all men. It is correspondingly one of the most serious contemporary expressions of Christian intellectual and spiritual capitulation that this particular truth should be so little reflected in current preaching and writing.[4]

Preaching about the judgment is unpopular; many people are repulsed by it. Others dismiss it as being much fury about nothing. To test these assertions, I selected homes in our community at random and asked people whether they thought there would be a final judgment. Forty percent responded that they either "suspect" or "are sure" the final judgment will *not* occur.

Since many present day preachers carefully avoid bringing up this undesirable subject, one can be certain that they are even more discrete about raising the most offensive aspect of the judgment, namely, hell. Regarding this silence, Richard Mouw wrote the following: "Whatever happened to hell? 'Hell seems to have cooled, waned, or even disappeared' in the thinking of contemporary Christians. At

4. Milne, *The Illustrated Bible Dictionary*, 839.

least that's what Dr. Martin Marty, a senior editor of *The Christian Century*, observes. . . . Most believers, whether pew sitters or professional theologians, no longer talk much about a God who damns people to eternal torment."[5]

Despite pastor's reluctance to talk about it, hell is dreadfully real. It was regarded as real and horrible in Old Testament times when the Hinnom Valley, the most putrid, gross, refuse dump of Israel was used to portray it.[6] Jesus also spoke of hell as very real and terrible, a place of torture where punishment never ended (Matthew 5:29–30; 10:28; 13:41–42; 18:8–9; 25:30, 46; Mark 9:43, 48; Isaiah 66:24).

Since judgment and hell truly exist, speak about them even though they might intimidate and offend.[7] Return to the Bible to discover the effect God intends the teaching of judgment and hell to have on His people. You will learn that its primary purpose, contrary to popular opinion, is to encourage believers in their service to God, *not* to make them worry that they have failed to do enough to merit God's favor.

The Warning that Creates Hope

As unlikely as it may seem, proclaiming the final judgment is a potent stimulant for engendering Christian hope. Accurate

5. Mouw, "The Waning of Hell," *The Banner*, 12.

6. Wieand, "Hinnom, Valley of," in *The International Standard Bible Encyclopedia*, 2:717–718.

7. Because honest talk about hell does raise genuine concern, you must have a well-articulated apologetic. One of the best I've heard was that of a first-generation Nigerian convert. He said, in respect to his ancestors, that he did not know their eternal destiny. If they were lost, they were condemned by a God who is infinitely more gracious than he himself could ever be. If they were saved, it was in and through the grace of God in Jesus Christ. In either case, the convert did not worry, for God would do what was loving, just, and right.

knowledge about God's judgment strengthens hope in two ways. First, it affirms that everyone who opposes God and lives defiantly in sin will receive His just and timely punishment. Second, it accepts God's declaration that everyone who trusts in the Lord for salvation should look expectantly beyond the sin, pain, and confusion of this world to God's reign of perfect peace and righteousness in glory.

Preachers who warn of eternal and dreadful punishment upon those who defy God and oppose Him and His church build confidence about the future in their listeners. Such pastors help true believers know God's mind and trust His Word for their own destiny.

Genuine hope requires accurate information about real danger. That is why, for example, cigarette packages carry warnings and street intersections have traffic lights. It's also why our federal government has often engaged in expensive media campaigns to inform the public about the threat of such diseases as AIDS (Auto Immune Deficiency Syndrome). Ignorance may sometimes be "bliss," but not when it is about actual, life-threatening dangers that can be avoided.

As a preacher, you have been schooled in the Word of God and are aware of the dangers of hell. If you fail to mention these perils to the people you serve, it can only mean that you don't really believe they exist. Otherwise, your concern for the unsaved and errant in your flock would be a façade. Preachers who deliberately keep the unsaved in the dark about the disaster that awaits them are negligent and culpable. Their silence is lethal!

According to Scripture, unfaithful spiritual shepherds who neglect to warn about danger will receive the very punishment their silence fails to predict (II Chronicles 19:10; Ezekiel 3:16–21; 13; 33:1–9). But those who are faithful are worthy of double honor and will save both themselves and their hearers (I Timothy 4:16; 5:17).

Since it is much more hopeful to be informed about danger than to be uninformed, preachers of hope must faithfully sound a piercing and unwavering note of warning.[8] When that note is heard by receptive ears, eternal catastrophe will be averted, the glory of God's justice will be honored, and believers will be strengthened to push forward in their service for the Lord even when the wind of opposition blows in their face.

Scripture gives many illustrations in both testaments of the encouragement God's people derive from the certainty of His judgment. Perhaps the most explicit examples are in the genre of biblical literature called the imprecatory psalms. In these shocking poems of predicted doom, people who plot, mock, and arm themselves against God and His anointed king are themselves ridiculed for their myopic vision and vanity.

We learn that the arrogant are foolish to ignore the wrath of a Holy God, for in righteousness He executes such ghastly punishment as to "cut off all flattering lips and every boastful tongue" (Psalm 12:3). How ill advised it is for them to turn their backs in sport on a God who is renowned as a sharp-shooting warrior (Exodus 15:3). In this regard, Psalm 64:5-9 offers a graphic description of the futility of all man-centered boasting:

> They encourage each other in evil plans, they talk about hiding their snares; they say, "Who will see them?" They plot injustice and say, "We have devised a perfect plan!" Surely the mind and heart of man are cunning. But God will shoot them with arrows; suddenly they will be

8. As I implied before in regard to Jonathan Edwards, warning should never sound alone. In Scripture, notes of warning are always harmonized with the more mellow and pastoral sounds of grace (Deuteronomy 11:26–32; Joshua 8:30–35; John 3:16–21; 5:24; Romans 8:1–4; I Thessalonians 1:9–10; 5:10; II Thessalonians 1:9–10).

struck down. He will turn their own tongues against them and bring them to ruin; all who see them will shake their heads in scorn. All mankind will fear; they will proclaim the works of God and ponder what he has done.

Because in imprecations the spirit of the poet was intertwined with the Spirit of God, these poems have amazing power to cure despair. As the psalmist looked at sinful pride with God's eyes and heard wicked sneers with His ears, the worshiper's heart quickly filled with outspoken confidence: God saw! God understood!

Because the psalmist was confident of the Lord's power to act, praise could begin. He did not have to wait for circumstances to change or enemies to retreat. Simply knowing what God would do was enough to turn groaning into rejoicing.

Psalm 64 illustrates this change in the poet's attitude. In this psalm, David opened with a complaint for protection (vs. 1), but closed a handful of verses later with an anthem of praise: "Let the righteous rejoice in the LORD and take refuge in him; let all the upright in heart praise him!"(vs.10). Why the change in the psalmist's tone? It's because God was revered as a perfect and invincible Judge.

In a form almost as graphic as the imprecations, the New Testament also teaches God's people to draw encouragement from their certainty of His judgment. For example, in the first chapter of Second Thessalonians, Paul urged perseverance in persecution and trials. Christians could endure hardships, for growing faith was clear evidence that God's judgment is right. It also verified that His people would be counted worthy of the kingdom of God for which they suffered. Consider the following words of Paul:

God is just: He will pay back trouble to those who trouble you and give relief to you who are

> troubled, and to us as well. This will happen
> when the Lord Jesus is revealed from heaven in
> blazing fire with his powerful angels. He will
> punish those who do not know God and do not
> obey the gospel of our Lord Jesus. They will be
> punished with everlasting destruction and shut
> out from the presence of the Lord and from the
> majesty of his power on the day he comes to
> be glorified in his holy people and to be mar-
> veled at among all those who have believed. (II
> Thessalonians 1:6–20)

Like Paul, Peter also referred to God's judgment as a reason to persist in hope. Speaking of the coming day of the Lord, the apostle said, "That day will bring about the destruction of the heavens by fire, and the elements will melt in the heat. But in keeping with his promise we are looking forward to a new heaven and a new earth, the home of righteousness" (II Peter 3:12–13).

One final reference to judgment as a stimulant to hope is found in the last chapter of the Bible, Revelation 22. There, with apocalyptic anticipation of the returning Judge, John prayed that the Lord Jesus will come soon (vs. 20).

These passages of Scripture and many others teach us how to preach the hope of the judgment. If people do not hear about the judgment, they are being deceived, and deep down they know it.

Chances for Heaven?

God condemns the guilty—only the guilty, and all of them. But the Lord acquits the righteous—only the righteous, and all of them. He never confuses the two groups. Therefore, those who have been clothed with the righteousness of Jesus Christ should take heart—that is, if they can be sure such righteousness is indeed theirs.

To raise the hope of heaven in your congregation, you need to help your members know which camp they are in—the guilty or the righteous. Determining this is a considerable problem for many people. According to a 1986 religious attitude poll,[9] seventy-two percent of Americans rated their own chances of going to heaven as "good-to-excellent." Eighteen percent were totally unsure; and even the seventy-two percent of relatively optimistic people spoke only of "chances" rather than assured knowledge. An examination of the results of more recent surveys[10] suggests that not much has changed in the nearly two decades since the original survey was done.

Consider a 35-year-old Baptist clerical worker from Indiana. While wavering in uncertainty, he explained that, "to go to heaven you have to be a good person, someone who is humble and doesn't just do good things to prove they're good. . . . My chances [of going to heaven] are kind of slim, maybe 50-50. You have to be more than a nice person. But, I'm still in the running."

Another person responding to the poll thought his chances of going to heaven were considerably higher. Based on his assumption that "the entrance exam won't be that tough," he believed his chances might run as high as eighty-five percent.

Sadly, the thoughts of the people polled for the 1986 survey continue to remain typical of our neighbors and perhaps even fellow church members. Some people regard the hope for heaven like a giant game of chance. They give life their best shot, shut their eyes in jittery wistfulness, and "hope" that after death they will open their eyes in heaven. Preacher, you must demonstrate that this type of "hope"

9. Survey conducted and reported in the December 1986 issue of *USA Weekend.*

10. As reported on various websites on the internet.

has *nothing* to do with biblical hope. Genuine Biblical hope is certain, error-proof, unshakable confidence in a God who cannot lie and cannot let those who belong to Him slip surreptitiously through His fingers (Romans 8:28–39; Philippians 1:6; I Peter 1:3–5).

When people think in terms of their "chances" for entering heaven, even if their "percentages" seem high, it is apparent that they do not understand the standard by which heaven is attained. Heaven is reserved for the *perfectly righteous*, not the only-slightly-tainted. Apart from Jesus Christ, the Righteous One, we are lost and doomed to hell. In Him we are saved, being clothed with His perfect righteousness. Without Christ, our chances of going to heaven are zero; but with Him, they are one hundred percent. That's not chance. That's absolute certainty!

How widespread is lack of assurance about going to heaven? It's very widespread, indeed! In the community survey to which I referred earlier, sixty percent of the people I contacted said they thought good works was the standard God would use to judge or evaluate us. Only five percent knew their eternal destiny would be determined on the basis of their association with Christ. Think of it! All the others were simply betting they would be accepted into heaven because they were "at least as good as most people" and that they had done "nothing really bad."

For your preaching to effectively help people move from doubt to certainty (or hope), you will have to clear up foggy thinking about the basis of salvation. You will also have to explain the difference between justification and sanctification.

Our Salvation and Our Righteousness

What is the basis of salvation? It is the grace of God in Christ (Ephesians 2:8–10; Romans 4:16; I Peter 2:24; 3:18). And what is grace? It is undeserved favor, the opposite of merit. Divine grace is a gift, not a wage.[11]

I well remember when the true meaning of God's grace dawned on me. I had been trying very hard to do what God wanted and to think pure thoughts. I was determined to serve God as well as I could, and I committed myself to Christ with as much resolve as I could muster. But almost before I could blink, I had again failed in my obedience to the Lord.

Then, one day, I had a God-inspired "bright idea!" I thought to myself, "In order to be acceptable to God, I'm going to have to trust in something other than my ability to achieve." That day, out of my failure and frustration, I thrust my whole weak, sinning self upon the Lord. I began to realize that my hope of heaven hung entirely on God's willingness to carry me to glory, rather than on my power to climb the ladder to its gates.

In his honest, true-to-experience style Lewis B. Smedes describes grace as having but one simple phrase in its vocabulary: "Accepted, you are accepted."

> The point is that the grace of God comes to us in our scrambled spiritual disorder, our mangled inner mass, and accepts us with all our unsorted clutter, accepts us with all our potential for doing real evil and all our fascinating flaws that make us such interesting people. He accepts

11. Though God's grace in Christ is the basis of our salvation, the Bible teaches with equal authority that we will be judged by our works (Matthew 16:27; 25:31–46; Romans 2:6; I Corinthians 3:8; Revelation 22:12). How can grace and works simultaneously serve as God's standard of judgment? Every person who is a recipient of God's saving grace is also a recipient of His sanctifying Spirit and, thereby, *will* at the time of judgment, be found to have Spirit-produced works of righteousness (see Galatians 5:16–18, 22-26; Ephesians 2:10; 5:18; Titus 2:11–14; James 2:14–26; I John 1:5–7).

> us totally as the spiritual stew we are. We are
> accepted in our most fantastic contradictions
> and our boring corruptions. Accepted with our
> roaring vices and our purring virtues. We are
> damaged masterpieces, stunted saints; there are
> ogres and angels in our basements that we can
> hardly tell apart and that we have not dared to
> face up to. For the whole shadowed self each
> one of us is, grace has one loving phrase: you are
> accepted. Accepted. Accepted. Accepted.[12]

When the reality of God's grace broke through to me, I discovered to my delight that my heart was at peace. Likewise, the hope of the glory ahead began to be a focused attraction in my life. With the basis of my salvation—God's grace—settled in my mind and heart, another question began to pester me. It was this: "How can my peace in Christ remain steady even when I discover fresh sins in my life?"

Troublesome as this question is, I found that it does have a satisfactory answer. And that answer, interestingly, is tied to a proper understanding of two uniquely biblical terms, *justification* and *sanctification*.

What do these unpopular, soul-settling terms mean? Justification is God's once-for-all act of *declaring* a person righteous in Christ. Sanctification is God's on-going work of *making* him or her holy. In other words, justification is God's work of stating what is true when we enter into Christ by faith. And sanctification is His work of making us resemble Christ in our daily lives.

In his book, *The Way of Holiness,* Kenneth Prior draws the following helpful distinctions between justification and sanctification:

> Justification deals with our condemnation in
> God's sight, while sanctification is His answer to

12. Smedes, *Shame and Grace,* 117

our sinful condition. . . . Justifying people does not affect their moral condition. When a judge declares someone, "not guilty," it is not reforming the prisoner. . . . [Justification is] legal, external, and objective, while sanctification, relating the purifying of heart and life, is experiential, internal, and subjective. Instead of being concerned with our outward standing, sanctification applies to inward condition. . . . And, there is another difference. A person is justified by a sovereign, once-for-all declaration of God the Father, just as a court of law makes a similar declaration concerning a defendant. Sanctification, however, is a gradual process which is effected by the inner working of the Holy Spirit. The process begins when the Holy Spirit first sets a sinner apart and imparts new life by the act of regeneration. It continues in the inward renewal of his nature. It is not completed until the end of this present life when he is glorified and made like Christ.[13]

Perhaps we could summarize the meaning of justification and sanctification in this way. Justification, or what God says about us, sets our destiny. Sanctification, or what God does in us, guides our behavior. It's easy to see that the two belong together. When the first happens, the second must follow.

God's redemptive work, once begun, will not stop until it is complete in the day of Christ Jesus (Philippians 1:6). He never starts with a bang and then loses interest. What begins in His mind ends in His glory for the golden links of His saving activity cannot be broken. (Romans 8:28–30; 16:20; I Thessalonians 5:23–24; II Timothy 4:18),

Preaching that presents God's saving work as an irreversible process creates hope and peace. It reminds believ-

13. Prior, *The Way of Holiness*, 61–64.

ers that they are people undergoing change. God is not yet through with them. Their faith is evidence that the Lord has started His work. The presence of ongoing sin makes it clear that He is not finished. Hope looks ahead to the day when His work will be complete.

Justification and sanctification preached with regularity and simplicity create a strong sense of security and hope. They are neither beyond comprehension nor superfluous. Rather, like the footings of a well-built house—they undergird.[14]

Eager for Judgment

Sincere yearning for God's judgment seems so extreme that you may imagine it to be a reality only for people who, for example, might experience the pain of intense injustice or religious persecution.[15] This should not be the case. No one who hears or assimilates hope-filled preaching should possess a blandly tepid interest in the return of Christ, the Judge. Both Scripture and Christian doctrine teach us that eagerness for judgment is right and normal for all believers.

14. For a thorough treatment of the theological concept of justification, see the following articles: Faulkner et al., "Justification," in *The International Standard Bible Encyclopedia*, 2:1168–1174; McGrath, "Justification," in *Dictionary of Paul and His letters*, 517–523; Packer, "Justification," in *Evangelical Dictionary of Theology*, 643–647. For a study of sanctification, see the following articles: Westerholm, "Sanctification," in *The International Standard Bible Encyclopedia*, 4:321–331; Porter, "Holiness, Sanctification," in *Dictionary of Paul and His Letters*, 397–402; White, "Sanctification," in *Evangelical Dictionary of Theology*, 1051–1054.

15. As indicated earlier, injustice and persecution are major biblical reasons for eagerness for judgment. Thus, preaching in socially hostile environments (as in many urban areas and in countries experiencing political oppression) is often dominated by themes of social justice and divine judgment.

Paul, as he wrote to the Corinthian believers, expressed confident enthusiasm about appearing with favor before the judgment seat of Christ. In fact, the apostle said that he preferred "to be away from the body and at home with the Lord" (II Corinthians 5:8). In II Timothy, which, we believe, Paul wrote shortly before being executed in Rome for his faith, he voiced a similar longing: "I have fought the good fight, I have finished the race, I have kept the faith. Now there is in store for me the crown of righteousness which the Lord, the righteous Judge, will award to me on that day—and not only to me, but also to all who have longed for his appearing" (4:7–8).

Peter, likewise, looked ahead with certainty and expectation to God's approaching Day of Judgment. The apostle's confidence rested on his familiarity with the Judge. Jesus, the person Peter preached, had been appointed by God as the Judge of the living and the dead (Acts 10:42; see Romans 2:16).

In the final Revelation of Jesus Christ an angel delivers similar messages of stern warning balanced by encouraging promises.

> To him who overcomes [the challenge to faith described by the angel], I will give the right to eat from the tree of life, which is in the Paradise of God. . . . He who overcomes will not be hurt at all by the second death. . . . To him who overcomes and does my will to the end, I will give authority over the nations—"He will rule them with an iron scepter; he will dash them to pieces like pottery"—just as I have received authority from my Father. . . . He who overcomes will, like them, be dressed in white. I will never blot out his name from the book of life, but will acknowledge his name before my Father and his angels. . . . To him who overcomes, I will give

> the right to sit with me on my throne, just as I
> overcame and sat with my Father on his throne.
> (Revelation 2:7, 11, 26–27; 3:5, 21)

Because anticipation and proclamation of final judgment was an essential teaching of the apostles, this subject naturally found its way into the church's earliest professions of faith. The Apostle's Creed, one of the most universally accepted Christian confessions, declares that Jesus "shall come [again] to judge the living and the dead." According the Heidelberg Catechism, this means the following for the believer: "In all my sorrows and persecutions, with uplifted head, I look for the very same Person who before offered Himself, for my sake, to the tribunal of God, and hath removed all curse from me, to come as Judge from heaven; who shall cast all His and my enemies into everlasting condemnation, but shall take me with all His chosen ones, to Himself into heavenly joy and glory."[16]

Note the positive, reassuring tone in the Heidelberg Catechism's description of the judgment. It conveys a sense of eagerness for the returning Judge. Believers who grasp the truth of the judgment will know why they can expect eternal life. They will trust the guarantee that their life's journey will end in the presence of God. They will also be assured that everyone who shuns the path of life and walks the road of sin and death will be condemned.

Preaching Judgment as a Message of Hope

How are you going to correct the popular misconceptions of the judgment through your preaching? Look to the Word of God and follow its guidance! It will lead you to warn

16. *Heidelberg Catechism*, Lord's Day XIX, Question and Answer 52. The entire catechism can be found at the Christian Classics Ethereal Library (CCEL) website: http://www.ccel.org/creeds/heidelberg-cat-ext.txt.

your congregation that the judgment is real and swiftly approaching. It will prompt you to unveil a coming event of unparalleled hope for all who believe. It will direct you to declare that when the Day of Judgment arrives, God will be vindicated, sin will be eliminated, suffering will be eradicated, injustice will be righted, and the church will be glorified.

The judgment is exceptional and unqualified good news. We should not shun it because the world ridicules it or because preaching it "might" produce fear.[17] The judgment is not a biblical scare tactic. It is a rainbow of promise painted by God on a darkened sky of sin.

17. Some people argue that talk about the judgment will precipitate sorrow and grief for believers who "see" relatives and friends condemned. Thus, their joy in Christ will drain away and they will be left empty and disheartened. Lewis, in *The Problem of Pain* offered a helpful response to that improper conjecture. He said that if this were the future of judgment-wise believers, God's plan and promise of heavenly joy and bliss for His children would be held captive by the unbelief of the condemned. But that cannot happen, for God will triumph, not unbelievers. In heaven, all anguish and misery will be done away, Satan will be defeated, and God will be all in all. Therefore, it follows that in glory, no memory of the unredeemed will plague the saints. Consider Isaiah 65:17–19, which says the following: "Behold, I will create new heavens and a new earth. The former things will not be remembered, nor will they come to mind. But be glad and rejoice forever in what I will create, for I will create Jerusalem to be a delight and its people a joy. I will rejoice over Jerusalem and take delight in my people; the sound of weeping and of crying will be heard in it no more."

CHAPTER EIGHT

Preaching Passages that Inspire Hope

IN THIS chapter, we will analyze eight representative preaching passages upon which messages of hope could be built and how you might communicate them to your congregation.[1] They deal with four basic types of distressing or threatening situations: persecution,[2] death, personal tragedy, and enticement to do evil. We will divide our study of each text into four sections: first, the troubling circumstance; second, the natural response; third, the divine encouragement; and fourth, the summary.

Hope in the Midst of Persecution: I Peter 1:3–9

The Troubling Circumstance

Peter wrote to believers in Asia Minor to encourage them to live victoriously in a hostile age. The Roman government, being suspicious of the church's talk about judgment and the overthrow of the existing world, turned from casual

1 My historical, theological, and Christological perspective for my comments on these passages has been greatly influenced by Cornelius Vanderwaal's commentary series entitled *Search the Scriptures*. Most of this material was originally published in Dutch under the title *Sola Scriptura* and translated into English by Theodore Plantinga.

2. In Scripture, persecution is the most frequently mentioned circumstance eliciting the encouragement of biblical hope.

indifference toward the followers of Christ to an attitude of open hatred.[3] This animosity eventually became so intense that it precipitated some of the most brutal persecution in the history of the church.[4]

3. It was not until the reign of Constantine in the early fourth century A.D. that Christianity was officially sanctioned by the Roman Empire. Prior to that time, Christianity was held in contempt by many government officials. Pliny the Younger (A.D. 61–113), the governor of the Roman province of Bithynia in Asia Minor from A.D. 111–113, wanted to know what his official stance should be toward Christians. He thus wrote a letter to emperor Trajan (A.D. 53–117) in which he asked for instructions. Pliny's letter indicates the kind of attitude that many Roman officials had toward early Christians: "I thought it . . . necessary . . . to find out finally what was true by putting to torture two girls who were called serving girls. But I found nothing but a depraved and enormous superstition. Consequently, I adjourned the investigation and turned to you for advice." (The full text of the correspondence between Pliny and Trajan can be found at the following Fordham University website: http://www.fordham.edu/halsall/ancient/pliny-trajan1.html.)

4. Tenny, *New Testament Survey*, 344. From the first through the third centuries A.D., Christians were repeatedly slandered and accused of wrongdoing by their opponents. In such an environment the behavior of Christians greatly affected the spread of the gospel. In his work entitled *Annals*, the Roman historian Tacitus (A.D. 56–120) described Christianity as a "deadly superstition." He also wrote that the emperor Nero (who reigned from A.D. 54–68), in an attempt to silence rumors that he had started the fire that destroyed much of Rome, blamed and punished Christians living in the city. (The full text of the *Annals* can be found at the following Internet Classics Archive link: http://classics.mit.edu/Tacitus/annals.mb.txt.) In A.D. 197, the early church leader Tertullian (A.D. 155–220) noted in his work entitled *Apology* some of the false charges leveled against believers. These included police and informers bringing up accusations against the Christians as sex criminals and murderers, blasphemers and traitors, enemies of public life, desecraters of temples, and criminals against the religion of Rome. (The full text of *Apology* can be found at the following link of The Tertullian Project: http://www.tertullian.org/articles/chevallier_apology.htm.)

Beaten and frightened, the church scattered throughout Asia Minor. But dispersion did not provide much relief.
Besides the loneliness of separation from their homelands,
believers were treated like resident aliens and were insulted
for the name of Christ.[5] Peter wanted to strengthen this
'"parish" of exiles', as Cornelius Vanderwaal calls them in
his commentary. As one who himself had given in when the
heat was on and had subsequently experienced God's forgiving and reinstating grace (Luke 22:31–32; John 21:15–17),
Peter was qualified to encourage others (I Peter 4:12–19).[6]

Christians living in North America today seldom experience interrogations, beatings, or imprisonment for their
faith. But they do face antagonism and feel the pressure of
ungodly opposition. This should come as no surprise, for
Scripture reveals that "everyone who wants to live a godly
life in Christ will be persecuted" (II Timothy 3:12; see John
15:18–19).

5. In *The Book of Revelation in Christological Focus*, Dan Lioy
notes that there is disagreement among scholars regarding the nature,
extent, and duration of the crisis that was experienced by believers in
the early church (p. 10). Some people go so far as to say there was no
form of empire-wide persecution, only incidental episodes of localized
harassment. But a candid and objective scrutiny of the evidence yields
the following opposite conclusions: 1. In the first century A.D., there
was an established pattern of Rome's persecution of the Jewish people;
2. The evidence from within the New Testament indicates that the
early church experienced persecution; and, 3. The historical reality of
this calamity is validated from ancient Roman and patristic sources
(pp. 11–12).

6. In I Peter 4:12, the apostle used the Greek noun πειρασμός
(*peirasmos*), which the NIV renders as "trial." It basically denotes
a testing of faith (Danker, ed., *A Greek-English Lexicon of the New
Testament and Other Early Christian Literature*, 793). For a detailed
discussion of the meaning of πειρασμός in this and related passages,
consult Seesemann, "*peirasmos*," in *Theological Dictionary of the New
Testament*, 6:29–30; and Louw & Nida, eds., *Greek-English Lexicon of
the New Testament: Based on Semantic Domains*, 1:332.

What trials for the faith do your people experience?[7] Sometimes opposition comes from within the church. When it does, it often appears as popular, twisted, half-truth or as schismatic, critical in-house bickering. In other situations, opposition comes from outside the church. Ridicule is one form of this opposition. When you, individually or collectively, personally or via mass media, are ridiculed as being naïve or narrow-minded, you are under attack for your faith.

Likewise, you could be threatened by possible legal action because you refuse to condone unbiblical sexual mores; or you might be made to pay for society's high-priced sexual revolution with its diseases, abortions, family disintegration, welfare costs, and psychological upheaval. Regardless of the situation, you are penalized by a requirement to support what you despise. Furthermore, when your time for worship is squeezed out by the advancing secularization of the Lord's Day and commercialization of religious holidays, you are victimized.

To identify current forms of persecution or trial with which you and your congregation are struggling, ask how the reign and ethic of Christ are challenged in your area or context. You will likely discover forms of opposition that are more subdued and sophisticated than those practiced during earlier periods of church history; even so, they may be equally as real and distressing as if they were whips and crosses.

Opposition to God and His people is here today and will continue until Christ returns (John 15:18–19; II Timothy 3:12–13; I Peter 4:12). Because the name of Christ necessarily causes those who refuse to listen to God's Word to stumble (I Peter 2:8; 4:13), even the most genteel

7. Scripture indicates that, while the type and intensity of persecution varies (I Peter 1:6; 5:10), the experience of intense persecution is not abnormal (4:12).

society will, upon occasion, lock horns and butt heads with the church.

The Natural Response

Natural responses to opposition include defensiveness, withdrawal, anger, and/or retaliation. It is not surprising, then, that Peter warned about these dangerous, unsanctified reactions. In particular, the apostle cautioned against the tendency to give up or be silent (I Peter 2:19; 3:15; 4:16, 19; 5:4, 9–10, 12), to fight back or be insubordinate (I Peter 1:13–15; 2:1–3, 11–12, 16; 4:1–4), and to bicker among themselves (I Peter 1:22; 3:8–9; 4:7–11).

The Divine Encouragement

How is it possible to be attacked by people and sifted by Satan, as Peter's dispersed congregation was, and remain resolute? It's by looking heavenward (John 14:1–3; I Peter 1:4; 3:4; 4:13; 5:1, 3, 6, 10). Preachers must urge congregations to fix their attention on an eternal reality that is unaffected by earthly conditions with its tendency to cause things to spoil, perish, or fade.

Peter knew that believers are controlled by what they gaze at.[8] He also understood that it's how people set their sails, not the gales themselves, that determine how individuals pass through the storms of life.[9] Pressing on through opposition, however, requires more than properly focused hope. The latter must be *living* and *vigorous*. After all, a hope that dies or fails when the going gets rough is useless. In contrast, valuable hope *lives*, for it continually

8. Lutzer, *How to Have a Whole Heart in a Broken World*, 27.

9. Ibid., p. 28. This figure is taken from a poem by Ella Wheeler Wilcox, whom Lutzer quoted. The writings of Wilcox can be found at the following website: http://www.ellawheelerwilcox.org/.

draws sustenance and energy from the permanently risen Jesus Christ.[10]

Summary

Concerned, witnessing Christians are ridiculed, persecuted, and hated. They are aliens amidst the philosophies and values of society. They prize righteousness, justice, and love above personal advancement and pleasure (I Corinthians 13:6). Therefore, they do not share many of their neighbors' interests.

Proper preaching of hope will fortify a congregation that is intimidated, challenged, or attacked by the world. Such preaching will also instill the truth that one day soon God will provide an eternal inheritance (I Peter 1:3–5). It will emphasize the promise that tests and trials are temporary (verse 6).

Peter's words in 1:3–9 relate to many of the themes we have developed in this book. The hope the apostle addressed is a God-centered confidence, not mere wishful human thinking. This hope focuses on the resurrection, produces new life here and now, awaits judgment, and expects eternal glory in Christ. Preaching such truth strengthens believers as they face persecution.

10. Consider the analogy of the branch and the vine Jesus used in John 15:4–5, "Remain in me, and I will remain in you. No branch can bear fruit by itself; it must remain in the vine. Neither can you bear fruit unless you remain in me. I am the vine; you are the branches. If a man remains in me and I in him, he will bear much fruit; apart from me you can do nothing."

Hope in the Midst of Social Injustice: James 1:2–4, 12

The Troubling Circumstance

There is much here in common with First Peter. Dispersion and oppression[11] had caused morale to wear thin.[12] James' frequent references to economic hardship, to social status, and to guarded, humble speech indicate that class distinctions had begun to cause disharmony and bitterness. Some were unjustly treated by heartless land barons (James 1:9–11; 5:1–6). Great patience and restraint was needed (5:7–11). Can preaching hope meet these circumstances? Nothing else can!

The Natural Response

The natural response to social injustice is to pay back in kind, resort to worldly tactics, or buckle under and support and imitate the oppressor. Many of the Jewish Christians to whom James wrote were shortsighted, for they had begun to respond in a hopeless manner. Also, though they were among the persecuted poor, some believers had begun to

11. In 1:2 and 12, James referred to these experiences as trials or testing of faith, and like Peter, he used the familiar Greek noun πειρασμός (*peirasmos*).

12. James evidently addressed his letter mainly to Jewish Christians both inside and beyond the borders of Palestine. This conclusion is supported by the following facts. James was an important leader in the Jerusalem congregation (Acts 12:17; 15:13–21; 21:18–25). He spoke to the recipients of his epistle as the "twelve tribes scattered among the nations" (James 1:1). This is terminology the nation of Israel cherished, even though it was fragmented (Matthew 19:28; Acts 26:7). James used Semitic syntax. Finally, he used Old Testament illustrations and Hebraisms (such as "Lord Almighty," which literally means "Lord of hosts," in 5:4).

insult other poor people (James 2:6), to show favoritism (verses 1–7), to slander (1:26; 3:1–12; 4:11; 5:9), and to covet and envy.

The Divine Encouragement

God's Word of encouragement in the Letter of James turns eyes from present grief to future glory. The Lord neither explains how to escape troubles nor offers cosmetic and momentary relief. Rather, He points through the pain of trial to the crown He will give those who pass the test.[13]

As a preacher who is called by God to encourage the distressed, tell your congregation the following: "With your crown assured, trials take on new meaning. They become catalysts to maturity and proofs of steadfastness (Romans 5:3–5). Those who endure are truly blessed, fortunate, and happy (Matthew 5:4, 10–12)."

Summary

God is just and fair, so preach it! People need to hear that truth again and again. Persecutors of God's righteous people will themselves reap trouble from the Lord at the judgment. Urge your listeners, therefore, to patiently endure suffering, weigh their words carefully, remain constant in love, and care for the weak and unfortunate.

This admonition is necessary, for people under stress tend to have short fuses and easily-raised hackles. Pressure, wrongly handled, may sour relationships and lead to self-centeredness. To remain balanced and determined, beleaguered Christians need the long look of hope that James prescribed.

13. See the following references to God's righteous judgment: James 1:2, 26; 2:12; 5:1–12.

Amy Carmichael, a missionary to south India, practiced that perspective. Against great odds, she fought forces of evil and rescued child prostitutes from temple service. What motivated her to boldly challenge sin and perversion? It was a single-minded hope for things eternal.[14]

Hope in the Midst of Antagonism and Disharmony: Philippians 1:27–30

The Troubling Circumstance

Chains clinked as Paul settled down to write his letter to the Philippians. The apostle was a prisoner because of his faith and hope in Christ (Acts 26:4–8).[15] Though bound physically, Paul's spirit and influence remained free and unfettered. In fact, chains could neither dampen his joy[16] nor restrain him from desiring and serving the advance of the gospel. The reason is that he had hope. Rather than de-

14. Skoglund, *More Than Coping*, 31.

15. When Paul said of his imprisonment that he was "put here for the defense of the gospel" (Philippians 1:16), he was specifically saying that God had brought him to Rome for a particular purpose. It was no accident or quirk of fate that he was there. In the approximately thirty years that had passed from Christ's resurrection to Paul's imprisonment, the gospel had been carried through incredible means from an obscure province of the empire—Judea—to the court of Caesar himself. Paul had been chosen to defend the truths of Christ in front of the most powerful and influential leaders of his time. The Roman world could reject the life-giving message Paul brought, but it could no longer ignore it.

16. *Joy* and its cognates appear sixteen times in Philippians! The focus is on the delight Paul had in serving Christ, regardless of the circumstances the apostle faced.

terring his mission, Paul's bonds promoted it (Philippians 1:12–14).

How did Paul's chains serve the progress of the gospel? To answer this question we must understand the kind and intensity of opposition that arose in Philippi. Judaistic legalism and antinomianism (chapter 3) had begun to confront and rival the gospel. It also seems from Paul's counterarguments in 3:12–21, that some were beginning to follow the Gnostic teaching of perfectionism "that eliminated the future hope of the Christians and transferred it to a present experience."[17]

As a result of this antagonism, the young Philippian church began to feel the heat of persecution (1:27–30). Despite the sting of hostility they encountered, Paul wanted the church members to shine like stars in a crooked and depraved generation (2:15–16) and stand firm in the Lord (4:1). Paul's chains were a clear and potent reminder of the distinctiveness of the gospel of grace and the need to persevere.[18]

---

17. Martin, *The Illustrated Bible Dictionary,* 1217.

18. Although we cannot be certain, it is likely that Paul's anticipation of continued ministry (Philippians 1:25–26) was correct and that he was able to visit Philippi again. Evidence from Scripture and statements from early Christian writers indicate that Paul was eventually released from the Roman imprisonment referred to in Philippians and at the end of the Book of Acts. The events surrounding the writing of what are called the Pastoral Letters (I and II Timothy and Titus) do not fit well with the events described in Acts and seem to indicate a release and future imprisonment in which the conditions were much worse for the apostle. In his Letter to the Romans, Paul declared his intention to take the gospel to Spain (Romans 15:24, 28). Statements from early Christian literature, apart from the Bible, indicate that Paul did succeed in reaching Spain. Such a trip would have had to come after the events recorded in the Book of Acts.

The Natural Response

We don't know the exact relationship between the introduction of false teaching, the threat of persecution, and the disharmony in the Philippian church, but we do know discord began to simmer among the saints. They were becoming testy (2:1–4, 14–16). Anxiety, rather than joy, was the result (4:2–4).

The Divine Encouragement

Paul showed that the way to correct emerging disunity, fear, and anxiety is to refocus our attention on Christ. Peruse Philippians and see how often renewed aim and perspective are commanded.

The Philippians had lost their point of concentration. Their minds, as citizens[19] of heaven had to be centered again on the hope of a returning Savior and on the eternal destiny His resurrection guarantees (Philippians 3:12–21). The churches' singularity of spirit and witness would be a "sign" to ungodly antagonists of their ultimate destruction, while to believers it would guarantee the hope of their salvation (1:27–30).

Summary

Hopeful, focused thinking is what your church needs when the screws of ungodly pressure tighten and when disharmony or schism erupts. Philippians 1:27–30 is a great passage of hope. Preach it to help those suffering for Christ view their plight as a privilege and a sign of future glory.

---

19. In Philippians 3:20, the Greek noun rendered "citizenship" is πολίτευμα (*politeuma*). It is derived from the noun πόλις (*polis*), which means "city" or "city-state" (Danker, *A Greek-English Lexicon of the New Testament and Other Early Christian Literature,* 844). In this verse Πολίτευμα refers to the believers "commonwealth in heaven" (p. 845).

Also, preach it to supply a reason for godly living when the going gets tough.

Hope in the Midst of Oppression: *Psalm 10*

The Troubling Circumstance

The psalmist complained of a two-fold problem: the arrogant were attacking the helpless and God had not intervened (see Habakkuk 1).[20] "Why has God remained distant?" the psalmist asked. "Why has He failed to act? Why has He ignored the pride of the wicked and the plight of the weak? Are not the crimes against the frail abrasive enough?"[21]

To urge God to act, the psalmist paraded the offenses of the wicked before the Lord's holy eyes: the haughty hunted the feeble as if they were prey; the boastful praised their own greed and despised the Lord; the self-reliant sneered at their enemies and congratulated themselves for their own invincibility; the vitriolic cursed, lied, and threatened; the sly lurked like cowards to destroy the innocent; and the

20. The opening verses of Habakkuk indicate a situation in which justice had essentially disappeared from the land. Violence and wickedness prevailed virtually unchecked. In the midst of these dark days, Habakkuk cried out for divine intervention (1:2–4). When the Lord responded that He would use the Babylonians to judge Judah (1:5–11), this created an even greater theological dilemma for Habakkuk (1:12—2:1). God's explanation that He would also judge the Babylonians (2:2–20) still left the prophet in a quandary. In Habakkuk's mind, an even larger issue than God's righteous response to evil was the vindication of His character (1:13). Through his interactions with the Lord, Habakkuk discovered that God's character is sovereign and holy. The prophet ultimately learned that God was not to be worshiped merely because of the temporal blessings He bestowed, but for His own sake (3:17–19).

21. These questions are a paraphrase of the biblical text.

celebrants of what had been gained through sinful practices convinced themselves that God had forgotten their sin.[22]

As a pastor, you can identify with the psalmist's complaint. Every day, you and your congregation experience or hear news of injustice and graft. Over and over greed is exalted.[23] Millions of innocent people are murdered (aborted), drugged (even grade-schoolers), and threatened (by crime, mail fraud, and so on). Even you feel the sting of sarcasm from the tongue of the world.

The prince of this age is plying his craft. Deceit, divorce, and divination are rampant. Drugs and disease are devouring human lives. Perhaps like the saints of old, you cry out, "Lord, how long? Don't you see? Won't you stop this terrible evil?"

The Natural Response

It is natural to cry out to God in grief.[24] The Lord expects and encourages us to do so. That's why God wanted the

22. The psalmist's words raise an important question about the problem of evil in the world. Note that evil is a lack of something that should be there in the relationship between good things. Whether one is considering wicked attitudes, actions, or aims, they result from the absence of the moral perfection that God originally intended to exist between good things. Ultimately, only God knows why He has allowed evil to exist in the world. He may use evil to bring home to us the distressing fact of our mortality, to warn us of greater evils, to bring about a greater good, or to help defeat evil. The last two reasons are especially evident in the cross of Christ. Despite the tragedy of the Messiah's suffering on the cross, His atoning sacrifice resulted in a greater good (the salvation of the lost) and the defeat of evil (for instance, sin and death).

23. A good example would be credit card commercials that equate what is "worldly" with what is "wonderful."

24. Other common responses to God's patience in the face of evil are to pout and run (consider Elijah, I Kings 19:3–5), abandon God and mock His inactivity (Isaiah 5:20–25; II Peter 3:3–7), and to think

psalmist's anguished cries of imprecation and lament and the acrid complaints of Habakkuk the prophet to be recorded.

The Divine Encouragement

In Psalm 10 and other imprecatory psalms,[25] God's method of encouraging those who see and feel the pain of evil is fascinating. First, He leads us to recite our grievances and express our pain. Next, He guides us to call upon Him to avenge Himself and redress the wrongs. Finally, He enables us to trust Him and praise Him for His power and love. Here is a clear-cut plan for a message on hope.

Why does God want us to call upon Him in this way? The reason is that by doing so, we join our hearts with the heart of God. The Lord sees what we suffer for His name and He grieves. He is just and will surely repay. Therefore, our hearts can take courage and rejoice in that hope.

Summary

Psalms of imprecation and lament are impassioned expressions of hope. To convey that hope to your congregation, you must first identify the suffering of the godly and because of it lead your people to cry out in anguish to God. Then, appeal to God to avenge Himself and establish His perfect righteousness, for He is holy and just. Next, lead your people to praise God, the eternal King, even before the wind of opposition has stopped blowing. Finally, relate your confidence in God to the work and reign of Christ.[26]

---

of God as being unfair (Psalm 73:13–14).

25. For further information on imprecatory psalms, see my discussion in chapter seven.

26. Since imprecatory psalms envision God's judgment, they naturally foreshadow the coming of Christ. For instance, Verses 14 and 16 of Psalm 10 point directly to Christ (see Philippians 2:9–11; I Peter 2:23).

Hope in the Midst of Death: John 11:25–26

The Troubling Circumstance

John 11:1 says that a man named Lazarus was sick. He lived in Bethany[27] with Mary and Martha, his sisters. Lazarus was so grievously ill that his sisters sent for Jesus (verse 3). They were convinced He could heal Lazarus, if He hurried to the scene (verses 21, 32). But from a purely human perspective, Jesus arrived too late. Lazarus died! Is this a passage from which to preach hope? Yes and here's why.

As we just noted, from our natural, human point of view, Jesus waited too long to heal Lazarus of his sickness. But Jesus appeared just in time to perform a more astounding miraculous sign (see 20:30–31).[28] Never before had He called a dead, decaying body from the tomb (17:11)! This was the Messiah's hour to reveal the hope-filled truth that, as Son of God, He Himself *is* the resurrection and the life (verse 25).

Jesus deliberately (11:7–8) and purposefully (verses 11–14) set out for Judea. Although He knew He would raise Lazarus from the dead, the Messiah still grieved (verse 35), for He loved Lazarus and hated death. Even in such an attitude there is hope!

---

27. Bethany was located about two miles southeast of Jerusalem on the eastern slope of the Mount of Olives (see John 11:18).

28. Miracles are events that unmistakably involve an immediate and powerful action of God, and these are designed to reveal His character and purposes. According to John 20:30–31, there were many signs that Jesus performed during the three years of His earthly ministry. John selected only seven miracles to discuss, and he used them to substantiate Jesus' claim to be the Messiah, the Son of God. Beyond that, the miracles showed that God is Lord over life and death, and over temporal and eternal matters.

Death is ugly. It's a fierce enemy that rips apart body and soul. It's cruel, especially as it terminates love and friendships. Death is relentless and tenacious. Anyone who has stood at the deathbed of a dear one knows that even when death is necessary to relieve pain, it is never a friend. Death is the wages of sin (Romans 6:23). It *must* be overcome or there is no hope.

In his honest, personal, passionate book, *Lament for a Son*, Nicholas Wolterstorff, Professor of Philosophical Theology at Yale Divinity School, unveils his conflicting and heart wrenching thoughts as he tries to cope with the accidental death of his 25 year old son, Eric.

> There's a hole in the world now. In the place where he was, there's now just nothing. A center, like no other, of memory and hope and knowledge and affection which once inhabited this earth is gone. Only a gap remains. A perspective on this world unique in this world which once moved about within this world has been rubbed out. Only a void is left. There's nobody now who saw just what he saw, knows what he knew, remembers what he remembered, loves what he loved. A person, an irreplaceable person, is gone. Never again will anyone apprehend the world quite the way he did. Never again will anyone inhabit the world the way he did. Questions I have can never now get answers. The world is emptier. My son is gone. Only a hole remains, a void, a gap, never to be filled.
>
> I skimmed some books on grief. They offered ways of not looking death and pain in the face, ways of turning away from death out there to one's own inner "grief process" and, on that, laying the heavy hand of rationality. I will not have it so. I will not look away, I will indeed re-

mind myself that there's more to life than pain.
I will accept joy. But I will not look away from
Eric dead. Its demonic awfulness I will not ig-
nore. I owe that—to him and to God. [29]

While the suffering and pain of death wrenched his
soul, Wolterstorff gradually experienced comfort and a
measure of relief in the suffering, death, and resurrection
of Christ.

> To believe in Christ's rising from the grave is to
> accept it as a sign of our own rising from our
> graves. If for each of us it was our destiny to
> be obliterated, and for all of us together it was
> our destiny to fade away without a trace, then
> not Christ's rising but my dear son's early dying
> would be the logo of our fate. Slowly I begin
> to see that there is something more as well. To
> believe in Christ's rising and death's dying is
> also to live with the power and the challenge to
> rise up now from all our dark graves of suffering
> love. [30]

The Natural Response

One of the most natural responses to tragedy and death is
to wonder what would have happened if circumstances had
been different. Mary and Martha had seen Jesus' power to
heal and, understandably, considered the difference Jesus'
presence might have made. "Lord, if you had been here,"
each of them said to Jesus, "my brother would not have
died" (verses 21, 32).

Were Mary and Martha's "if only . . ." remarks subtle
accusations against God, or were they simply recognition

29. Wolterstorff, *Lament for a Son*, 33,54.
30. Ibid., 92.

of Jesus' power? Whatever the case, their words indicate that they had not yet fully accepted Lazarus' death. They felt helpless and anguished. Why did this tragedy have to happen, they seemed to reason, if Jesus could have been prevented it?

The Divine Encouragement

Martha's anguish, though welling from a spring of sorrow, rippled over a rock of confidence and hope, for she believed in the resurrection (John 11:24)! In fact, her words, "that even now God will give you whatever you ask" (verse 22), suggest Martha may have expected Jesus to raise Lazarus right then and there.

Jesus' response about being "the resurrection and the life" (verse 25) perhaps disappointed Martha. She had hinted at immediate action, but Jesus seemed to give her a theological principle. Although Jesus' words may have been less than what Martha desired, they established the only solid foundation upon which can be built the hope of eternal victory over death. And it is your basis for preaching hope in the midst of grief.

The strongest encouragement anyone can give the dying and grieving is to point them to Jesus, for He is "the resurrection and the life." The personal application of this encouragement relates to the whole person, both the physical and the spiritual. It is eternal, and it is the hope that weak, fragile mortals need to hear.

How can preaching John's account of the resurrection of Lazarus encourage those to whom you minister? It can do so in the following ways: first, by pointing to the One who is Himself the resurrection and the life; second, by showing that believers can live, even though they die; third, by helping them see that death is not final; yes, it is savage and destructive, but it is not the end for those who die in Christ;

and fourth, by giving actual, historical verification of the truth of Jesus' messianic claims.

Summary

John knew that Jesus is the Christ, the Son of the living God (John 20:31). The apostle had watched the Messiah, followed Him, loved Him, revered Him, and believed in Him. John wanted others to do the same (I John 1:1–4).

In his Gospel, John recorded one miraculous sign after another and added proof after proof, to convince his readers to believe in Jesus and receive eternal life (John 1:12; 3:16). The most amazing of all those signs was the resurrection of Lazarus. By that sign Jesus demonstrated convincingly that all hope for the dying resides in Him. Your people and their relatives and friends are dying! Preach Christ, the resurrection and the life, and you will give them hope!

Hope in the Midst of Grief:
I Thessalonians 4:13–18

The Troubling Circumstance

Death has no favorites. It strikes all alike, even believers who expect the Lord's return. This fact caught the Thessalonian Christians by surprise. They seem to have thought that the Messiah would return before any of their numbers had died.

We can easily understand this incorrect assumption. Jesus (Matthew 24:43; Luke 12:39–40), Peter (Acts 3:21), and Paul (17:31) had all spoken of the Lord's return as a sudden, decisive, and cataclysmic event. Furthermore, Paul's theology was definitely Parousia-oriented.[31] He insisted that

31. In the letter of I Thessalonians alone, there are eight references

believers keep an eye on heaven as they serve the Lord on earth (I Thessalonians 1:9–10; 2:12, 14–16; 3:13; 4:6, 13—5:11, 23), and that they try, through their serving, to give earth some of the flavor of heaven (see Matthew 6:10).

The Natural Response

If the Lord's return would bring about the glorious future that the Thessalonian believers thought it would, they would naturally be troubled to think that their loved ones and friends died without experiencing it. Therefore, much like their pagan neighbors, they began to grieve and mourn in hopeless despair.

Paul responded by teaching his readers that there are two kinds of grief—hopeless grief and hopeful grief. They are very different one from the other. Hopeless grief is godless. It is an empty, cavernous, and inconsolable anguish. It is a sigh of despair with no future. It sees no purpose, finds no answers, and discovers no relief.

Hopeless grief was what we saw the believers in gods and spirits in Taiwan experience when their loved ones died. They wept and howled as those who had no hope. Hopeless grief wears a dismal, desperate, dark face. Wherever it appears it always bears the mark of empty pain.

Hopeful grief is quite different. Although it too suffers pain, it looks beyond the anguish of the moment to life in the glorious presence of God and sees a brilliant future. As it weeps, it smiles; and as it cries, it exclaims, "'Where, O death, is your victory? Where, O death, is your sting?' The sting of death is sin, and the power of sin is the law. But thanks be to God! He gives us the victory through our Lord Jesus Christ" (I Corinthians 15:55–57).

---

to the Lord's return and the glory surrounding it.

The Divine Encouragement

To encourage the Thessalonians to look beyond death, Paul taught them that Christ would return to earth like a dignitary from a foreign land. When He comes, He will call and meet the citizens of heaven in the air. Both believers who already have died and we who are still alive will hear Him and go to welcome and honor Him. And so, we will "be with the Lord forever" (I Thessalonians 4:17). This truly is the blessed hope![32]

Summary

Do you want to preach hope when the saints die? Listen to Paul and preach his message of the Lord's return. There is hope! Jesus lives and is coming to reign. Death is not final and the grave is not permanent. Do you preach this message? Do your people look for the Lord to return? Do they know they will rise from the grave? Are they ready to meet the Lord in the air? Do they encourage each other with Paul's words?

32. Contrary to popular notions, Paul taught that it is possible to have hope in the face of death. Believers have a well-founded belief that the dead in Christ are now safely and happily with the Lord. In this context, then, it is appropriate that Paul compared dying to falling asleep. The comparison suggests that death is not the end of all existence. The raising of the bodies of dead believers is like waking from sleep. Furthermore, Christ's resurrection—the guarantee of the believer's resurrection—was no fairy tale. Jesus clearly survived death, and the survival of believers beyond the grave is equally certain. The Thessalonians could expect to see their departed loved ones again—in the company of the Lord.

Hope in the Midst of Tragedy:
Job 1:20–22; 2:10; 42:1–6

The Troubling Circumstance

"Fasten your seatbelts. We're about to hit turbulence!" That's the warning we hear before a plane passes through rough air. For most of life's rough spots there are no warnings. They simply strike and leave us numb and shaken.

That's how it was with Job. He was righteous. He was rich. He had family and friends. His life was in order. Then tragedy hit and he was ruined. In a relatively short span of time, his vast wealth, his servants, his much-loved children, and eventually his health were all snatched from him. He was left a loathsome, smelly, hen-pecked and friend-pecked man sitting alone atop an ash heap, scraping his sores with a piece of broken pottery.

Job's anguish is classic. Few people in the world have ever known such grief. Job's response is also classic. To the first series of calamities he responded, "Naked I came from my mother's womb, and naked I will depart. The Lord gave and the Lord has taken away; may the name of the Lord be praised" (Job 1:21).

Then, when his health failed and his wife verbally attacked him, Job replied, "You're talking like a foolish[33] woman. Shall we accept good from God, and not trouble?" (2:10). We learn that "in all this, Job did not sin by charging God with wrongdoing" (1:22; see 2:10). How could this beleaguered man endure? It was because he had hope.

---

33. Concerning Job 2:10, the *Net Bible* offers this clarifying thought: "The word 'foolish' (*nabal*) has to do with godlessness more than silliness (Ps. 14:1). To be foolish in this sense is to deny the nature and the work of God in life its proper place."

The Natural Response

Our natural response to tragedy often follows the pattern of Job's grief. Our initial reaction is resigned acceptance. "Well," we say, "I couldn't do a thing about it. That's just the way it is." Before long, however, anger, frustration, and pain set in and erupt into nagging doubt and even accusation. In Job's case, his inner turmoil was fueled by the charges of his wife and friends.

Eventually, because Job lost hope, he lashed out at God: "May the day of my birth perish, and the night it was said, 'A boy is born!' That day—may it turn to darkness; may God above not care about it; may no light shine upon it" (Job 3:3–4). Later in the book we read these words: "Even if I summoned [God] and he responded, I do not believe he would give me a hearing. He would crush me with a storm and multiply my wounds for no reason. He would not let me regain my breath but would overwhelm me with misery" (9:16–18).[34]

34. In some respects, the Book of Job is a long answer to a pointed question: if God is the sovereign Lord of the universe, then why does He allow suffering to come to the godly and good fortune to the wicked? For Job, thinking about this question moved into a consideration of the nature of God. In the face of Job's multiple calamities, he was forced to examine the foundations of his faith and to scrutinize his concept of the Lord. Thus Job found himself struggling with this question as well as with his counselors' traditional answers to it. His counselors' primary view, stated and discounted in the book, was that human suffering is a direct result of sin. They believed that God punishes the wicked in this life by sending affliction, and that He rewards the righteous in this life by providing blessings. But such a view did nothing to clear up Job's perplexity, since he knew he was a righteous man and had done nothing to earn the suffering he endured. Job was, in fact, afflicted in numerous ways as a test of his faithfulness to the Lord. And yet he was apparently oblivious to the fact that he was the object of that test—one God Himself had permitted after being challenged by Satan. Finally, God came out of a whirlwind and gave Job an answer to all his questions: trust the Lord regardless

Job's problem, says Charles Ohlrich, was that "God appears omnipotent . . . but not just."[35] To Job, God's assault was unreasonable. Accusatory as he was, what Job really wanted was "an unveiling of God's heart, a vision of His face. In the midst of evil (he) want(ed) to find goodness in God, in the midst of ugliness, (he) long(ed) for a vision of beauty in God, and by means of this discovery and this vision (he) want(ed) to transcend the evil and ugliness which engulf(ed) (him)."[36]

The Divine Encouragement

How encouraging that God accepted Job despite his complaint! God also knows and cares for your people when they cry out to Him, even when their cry is bitter and flawed. But God does more than patiently listen. He also helps with our mental distress by confronting us with His greatness and silencing us by His glory (Job 38–41). When you preach the Lord as He is, people will bow their proud heads before Him (42:1-6) and know that the reasons for pain are hidden in God's own righteous mind (see John 9:3).

Summary

The hope that Job discovered can be found only when God is seen in His creative glory. Before His majesty our attacks against His justice and our impunging of His goodness cease.

---

of the present circumstances. For Job to achieve godly wisdom, he was to trust in the almighty, infinite Creator, whose wisdom and ways were far beyond what he could imagine. In the end, all of Job's understanding, reason, and doubt had to give way to faith.

35. Ohlrich, *The Suffering God*, 21.
36. Ibid., 25. See also Job 13:24.

In a world of travesty and suffering proclaim that God's plan is righteous and unfailing (Job 42:2; Romans 8:18–39).

Hope in the Midst of Enticement to Do Evil: Titus 2:11–14

The Troubling Circumstance

Churches on the island of Crete were being deceived by self-centered, nit-picking Judaistic leaders who were more interested in religious trivia and profiteering than in godliness (Titus 1:10–16). Their divisive teaching was ruining whole households, and the church was beginning to disintegrate.

In order to stop the evil infesting the churches, Paul issued the following directives to Titus. First, either silence or cut off warped[37] and disruptive leaders (1:11, 13; 3:10–11). In their place, install disciplined, temperate elders who hold firmly to the revealed Word. Second, teach various groups in the church how to behave so they will have maximum positive influence for Christ in the world (2:1—3:2). And third, stress the grace of God in Christ, and show how it relates to godliness and the hope of the appearance of our great God and Savior, Jesus Christ (2:11–15; 3:3–8).

---

37. For Paul, heresy was not simply a matter of differing opinions about the interpretation of Scripture. While there was clearly a doctrinal component to the problem of heresy, at the root of it was a matter of the heart. According to Paul, a heretic was one who was "warped" (Titus 3:11) or more literally, "turned aside." The church was not to shy away from excluding those who stubbornly promoted false teaching, since their refusal to accept the patient correction of the church's leaders rendered them "self-condemned." They were not merely mistaken; they were hardened in rebellion against the truth. Ultimately, a rejection of God's truth was a rejection of God.

The Natural Response

The natural response to corrupt leadership in the church is permissiveness, apathy, and laziness. If poor, ungodly leaders trouble your church in one way or another, you must quiet or dismiss them. Your church is only as strong as its leaders. Remember that wherever the door of easy religion opens, some will almost certainly enter. How enticing it appears to live "freely" in sin and yet claim the favor of God! Even in churches where the gospel is faithfully preached, there is always pressure for cheap grace.

Preacher, your task is not easy. You must point out that faith without works is dead. You need to speak the Word of the sympathetic High Priest to those who are being sanctified, not the words of a "sympathetic psychiatrist" to those who are satisfied with living in sin.

The Divine Encouragement

How can you give genuine hope to believers who are tempted? It is by showing the inconsistency of waiting for Christ—our blessed hope—while living recklessly in sin. True knowledge of the grace of God in Christ provides both the reason and the will to refrain from ungodly behaviors and worldly passions. It sensitizes us so we abhor the sin for which Christ died and desire the holiness that He promises to create within us.

Grace always promotes godliness and never destroys it. You can identify people who live in grace by their desire for heaven. They are clearly people-in-waiting, people longing for their Redeemer and Purifier. Preacher, "these, then, are the things you should teach. Encourage and rebuke with all authority. Do not let anyone despise you" (Titus 2:15).

Summary

If the stability of your church is eroding because of corrupt or spiritually unqualified leaders, you must take action before it's too late. You must appoint godly leaders who can impact your church for good, and you must teach church members the proper understanding of grace and holiness. When you do, your people will gain hope, say "no" to sin and "yes" to the appearance of their Lord and Savior, Jesus Christ.

Epilogue

IN THE previous chapters we noted that modern preaching generally and woefully fails to incorporate a biblical perspective of hope. We also discovered that ministers with a human-centered theology offer their congregants a mere panacea for their discouragement and despair. Against this backdrop, I have shown how you can preach in a way that will foster hope among members of your congregation and at the same time exalt Christ.

We began our journey by taking aim at biblical despair (chapter one). This is an important starting point, for every believer encounters challenges, frustrations, and opposition. In fact, on the average, it seems, at least one-third of a gathered congregation on any Sunday comes to worship in varying degrees of discouragement, depression, or despair.

If such despair is left unchecked, it can suck the spiritual life out of your congregation. And as we noted, the solution is to refocus the attention of believers on God-given hope. With it they are able to thrive, grow, and press ahead. Such hope is based on the victory of the cross and energized by the promise of the resurrection. Believers who are downcast can rest assured that the Messiah who reigns and the God who rules is not distant or uncaring; rather, He is present among them and faithful in His love for them.

In the second chapter, we focused our attention on the specific target of biblical hope, which is the resurrection from the dead and the return of Jesus Christ. That hope is neither groundless optimism nor wishful thinking laced with doubt. Rather, what we hope for is absolute and sure because we wait for that which God has promised. We who have a truly biblical hope are confident of a certain and glorious future in the Savior. This assurance is anchored like steel shafts driven into the solid rock of God's person and His Word.

Depressed, despondent, lonely, and suffering people need to be reminded of the truth of the Messiah's return. They must also be told that the God of history is steadfast and reliable. When they hear these truths preached, they'll take heart. Moreover, people will rejoice in knowing that God is strong and eternally present. When we proclaim Him, we surely bring confidence and joy to our people.

Chapters three and four examined incomplete views of hope. We noted that many people today are ignorant of how to consider their daily struggles in the light of the return of Jesus and His emerging kingdom. Instead, they are bowing before the shrines of feel-good, positive thinking, New Age spirituality, seeker-sensitive re-envisioning of the old fashioned gospel of grace, dispensational premillennialism, and theological liberalism.

In contrast to the human-centered forms of hope arising from these views, a God-centered hope acknowledges the sovereignty of the Lord and affirms that not one of His promises will ever fail. Adherents realize that God alone creates reality and acts in all-powerful might to sustain it and bring it to a satisfying consummation at the end of the age. In short, the focus of believers is on the Parousia of Jesus Christ and eternal life in the presence of our holy, almighty God.

Preachers of biblical hope are absolutely convinced that Jesus arose, ascended to the Father's right hand, and will come again in great power and glory. Furthermore, they know that to proclaim such hope is to declare good news about what has happened in history and about what will take place in the world to come. This is why they believe their labor in the Lord is not in vain.

Chapters five, six, and seven function as a counterweight against the incomplete views of biblical hope covered in chapters three and four. In chapter five, the emphasis is on preaching the hope of the kingdom of God. We noted that the Lord not only rules, but also that His rule is spiritual. In terms of the latter, while the kingdom's "center of activity" is spiritual and internal, this characteristic does not exclude physical manifestations.

Your people will be encouraged when you preach the good news that the King of heaven is already on the march. In fact, the Lord has already begun to conquer His enemies and will soon destroy every opponent. And because the kingdom has already arrived in provisional form, it means our Christian experience today relates directly to kingdom life in the world to come. It also means that our fear of death should be replaced with anticipation of glory.

Pastor, it really is possible for us to begin to live the life of eternity, the life of heaven, right now in and through our daily activities. Heaven can touch earth in our presence, and our lives can begin to actually reflect the glory of God. Preaching the Christian life as a foretaste of heaven is wonderful and satisfying. It provides incredible joy, offers peace beyond understanding, and gives meaning to every breath of life. But such preaching does more than that. It replaces the fear of death with an anticipation of glory.

The grand truths of chapter five are reinforced in chapter six, which discusses preaching the hope of the presence of God. To be in His presence is to be close enough to Him to see Him as He is and transparent enough to invite Him to see us as we are. At first, a real encounter with the Lord produces repentance. Then, as we bow in awe before Him, we sense that the very power and glory of God that made us tremble has become our protective shield.

Since believers already have begun to experience the initial fulfillment of the promise of God's abiding presence, we look forward in eager hope to the event that will bring about the full realization of that promise, the Parousia. Indeed, to be near God and enjoy uninhibited fellowship with Him is the goal of the Christian life. It is also the basis for biblical hope.

When you hold these truths before your congregation, they will be spurred on by what they already know and possess. In addition, preaching that declares the Bible's hope liberates believers to expect the blessings in store for those upon whom God's face shines and His favor rests.

Preaching the hope of the judgment of God, which is the focus of chapter seven, rounds out the discussion begun in chapter five and continued in chapter six. At first it might seem odd to equate divine judgment with hope. But for true, born-again believers, the judgment is *good* news.

In point of fact and contrary to popular opinion, the primary purpose of the Bible's teaching about judgment and hell is to encourage believers in their service to God, *not* to make them worry that they have failed to do enough to merit God's favor. Moreover, it's a fountainhead of encouragement and a stimulant to godliness, not a source of despair or terror. That's why, with the proper emphasis on God's grace, judgment can be preached hopefully.

Preachers who warn of eternal and dreadful punishment for those who defy God and oppose Him and His church build confidence in believers about the future. These ministers help true Christians know God's mind and trust His Word for their own destiny. Believers not only are taught to trust in the Lord for salvation, but also to look expectantly beyond the sin, pain, and confusion of this world to God's reign of perfect peace and righteousness in glory.

Because this book is designed for both pastors and lay church leaders, it does more than just present a theological understanding of biblical hope. It also has plenty of suggestions for preaching hope directly and indirectly. While we have seen this here and there in the previous chapters, all of chapter eight is devoted to hope-inspiring preaching passages.

It is at this point that considerable time and attention is devoted to analyzing eight representative Scripture passages of hope. And we discover that, to preach hope effectively, we must be able to identify and communicate the following: first, what the troubling circumstance of the passage is and how it relates to our present-day situation; second, what the natural response to this circumstance is and how it is inadequate and futile; and third, what the hope of the gospel is and how it relates to a future in Christ. Preacher, when you offer biblical hope, you can expect your people to be encouraged even in the eye of life's storm.

In conclusion, hope is faith looking forward. Which way does your preaching look? Ahead? If so, how far? Only biblical hope, focused on the resurrection and affirmed by the renewing Holy Spirit, can change us internally and provide life for a future in the presence of the living God.

My purpose in writing this book has been to encourage you to preach with uplifted head in eager expectation of what lies further on in Christ, and to teach your congregation to embrace the same perspective.

Important Preaching Passages of Hope

ALTHOUGH ONLY some of the passages in this list make direct reference to hope, all of them help create within the people of God, eager anticipation of what He ultimately will accomplish through Christ. Since the categories under which the texts are placed are broad and general, a great variety of specific concepts are included under each one. As you read these passages and others, you might wish to expand the list or create your own. Some of the pericopes listed obviously contain far more material than can or should be expounded in one message or lesson.

Hope for the Righteous Kings' Reign

Genesis 35:11–15
Genesis 49:8–12
I Samuel 8:10–18
I Samuel 12:8–15
I Samuel 15:22,23
II Samuel 7:18–29
I Chronicles 17
I Chronicles 18:6b
II Chronicles 6:16,17
II Chronicles 7:17–22
II Chronicles 20:1–30
Psalm 2, 10, 24, 45, 47, 93, 98
Isaiah 52:7–12
Jeremiah 33
Ezekiel 37:15–28

Daniel 2:44, 45
Daniel 4:2, 3
Daniel 7:1–14, 23–27
Amos 9:11–15
Obadiah 17, 18, 21
Zechariah 14: 9–21
Matthew 16:13–28
Matthew 21:1–11
Matthew 22:41–46
Matthew 26:6–13
Matthew 28:16–20
Acts 9:1–19
Acts 13:13–41
Romans 16:25–27
I Timothy 6:11–16
II Peter 1:10, 11
Hebrews 1:1–3, 8–10
Hebrews 2:5–8a
Revelation 1:4–8
Revelation 5:5–14
Revelation 7:9,10
Revelation 11:15–19
Revelation 12:10–12
Revelation 17:12–14
Revelation 19:11–16
Revelation 20:7–15

Hope for God's Righteous Judgment

Leviticus 10:4–7
Numbers 14:20–25
II Kings 17:7–20
Psalm 9, 11, 22, 31, 37, 41, 50, 58, 62, 76, 110
Isaiah 24:14–16a
Isaiah 26:1–15

Isaiah 40:9–11
Isaiah 42:1–9
Isaiah 45:18–25
Jeremiah 47:27–28
Joel 2:28–32
Habakkuk 3:16–19
Matthew 5:17–48
Matthew 13:47–50
Matthew 23
Acts 7:56
Romans 1:18—2:16
II Peter 3:1–13
Revelation 19:1–5

Hope for Protection and Eternal Life in God's Presence

Genesis 15:1–3
Exodus 29:38–46
Deuteronomy 12:1–15, 17–22, 26–28
Deuteronomy 31:7, 8
Joshua 1:1–9
II Chronicles 6:10, 11
Psalm 5, 16, 23, 27, 42, 43, 52, 61, 84, 91
Isaiah 4:2–6
Ezekiel 43:1–12
Ezekiel 48:35b
Joel 3:17–21
Zephaniah 3:14–17
Matthew 21: 12–17
I Peter 1:3–5
Hebrews 6:13–20
Jude 24, 25

Hope for God's Mercy
—the Forgiveness of Sins

Genesis 3:14–19
Exodus 34:1–7
Numbers 14:13–19
II Chronicles 6:18–42
II Chronicles 7:11–17
Ezra 10:1–17
Nehemiah 9:1–37
Psalm 25, 32, 38, 51, 53, 65, 73, 103, 130
Isaiah 52:13—53:12
Jeremiah 31:31–40
Ezekiel 36
Hosea 11, 14
Zechariah 13:1
Matthew 26:17–30
Mark 2:1–17
Luke 15:11–32
Luke 18:9–14
Luke 19:1–10
John 1:29–34
Hebrews 4:11–16
Jude 17-21

Hope for God's Unfailing Love
and Constant Care

Genesis 12:2,3
Genesis 17:1–14
Exodus 3:7–9
Exodus 6:2–9
Deuteronomy 10:14–11:1
Deuteronomy 26:16–19
I Kings 8:22–30, 56–61

II Chronicles 6:14,15
II Chronicles 34:29–33
Psalm 33, 100, 117, 138, 147
Isaiah 40:25–31
Ecclesiastes 3:19–27
Jeremiah 29:10–14
Hebrews 7:23–28
I John 3:16–18
I John 4:7–19

Hope for Life beyond Death

Genesis 5:21–24
Job 19:23–27
Isaiah 26:19
Ezekiel 37:1 –14
Matthew 20:17–19
Matthew 22:23–33
Matthew 26:31–35
Matthew 28:1–10
Mark 5:21–43
Mark 16:1–8
Luke 16:19–31
Luke 24:1–12, 36–53
John 11:17–44
John 20:1–9
Acts 2:22–40
Acts 3:11–16
Acts 5:29–32
Acts 17:1–4, 18, 31
Acts 23:6
Acts 26:22, 23
Acts 28:20
I Corinthians 15

Colossians 1:3–8
Revelation 1:17, 18

Hope for Wisdom, Truth, Grace, and Life from God

II Chronicles 1:8–10
II Chronicles 2:11, 12
Proverbs 8:22–36
Proverbs 23:15–18
John 1:14–18
John 3:16–21
John 5:16–30
John 6:25–59
Romans 1:1–6
Romans 4:18–5:5
I Corinthians 1:18–2:16
II Corinthians 3:7–4:12
II Corinthians 5:1–10
Colossians 2:9–15
Colossians 3:1–4
Titus 1:1–4
II Timothy 1:1
I John 1:5–7
I John 5:10–12, 18–20

Hope for the Coming and/or Return of the Messiah

Exodus 12:1–13
Leviticus 16:15–17
Numbers 21:7–9
Numbers 24:14–25
Psalm 22, 87

Isaiah 11:1–11
Isaiah 61:1–9
Ezekiel 34
Micah 5:1–5
Zechariah 3
Matthew 1:18–25
Matthew 24
Matthew 25:1–13
Luke 1:26–38
Titus 2:11–15
James 5:5–11
I Peter 1:13–21
Hebrews 9:23–28
Hebrews 10:19–11:3
Hebrews 12:25–29
I John 2:29–3:3

Hope for Future Glory

Numbers 23:6–10, 17–24
Numbers 24:1–9
Deuteronomy 28:1–14
II Chronicles 5:13b–14
II Chronicles 7:1–3
Isaiah 25:1–8
Isaiah 35
Isaiah 55:12–13
Isaiah 60:18–22
Ezekiel 47:1–12
Micah 4
Haggai 2:6–9
Matthew 17:1–11
Luke 2:21–40
John 14:1–4
John 17:20–26

Romans 6:1–14
Romans 8:18–39
Romans 15:1–13
I Corinthians 1:4–9
Galatians 1:3–5
Ephesians 1:11–2:10
Philippians 1:3–11, 18b–26
Philippians 3:12–16
Colossians 1:24–29
I Timothy 3:14–16
II Timothy 2:8–13
II Timothy 4:6–8
James 2:1–7
I Peter 4:12–19
I Peter 5:1–4, 8–11
II Peter 1:10, 11, 16–18
Hebrews 2:5–18
Hebrews 12:1–3
Revelation 21:1–5

Hope for the Shalom of Christ

Isaiah 2:2–4
Isaiah 9:7
Isaiah 11:6–9, 14
Isaiah 32:1
Isaiah 45:11
Isaiah 60:3–5, 14
Isaiah 66:20
Matthew 8:14–17, 23–27
Matthew 10:25–30
Matthew 14:13–21
Matthew 18:1–9
Matthew 20:29–34
Mark 10:13–16, 35–45

Luke 2:8–20
John 13:1–17
John 16:17–33
Romans 13:8–14
Philippians 4:8–9
Colossians 1:15–20
Colossians 3:12–17
Revelation 21:9–14, 22—22:5

Bibliography

Bauckham, R. J. "Moltmann, Jürgen," in *New Dictionary of Theology*, S. B. Ferguson and D. F. Wright, editors. Downers Grove, Illinois: InterVarsity, 1988.

Beker, J. Christian. *Paul's Apocalyptic Gospel: The Coming Triumph of God*. Philadelphia, Pennsylvania: Fortress, 1982

Benson, B. E. "Postmodernism," in *Evangelical Dictionary of Theology*, Second Edition, W. A. Elwell, editor. Grand Rapids, Michigan: Baker Book House, 2001

Berkhof, Hendrikus. *Well-Founded Hope*. Richmond, Virginia: John Knox, 1969.

Bible. *New International Version*. Grand Rapids, Michigan: Zondervan Publishing House, 1985.

Boettner, Loraine. *The Meaning of the Millennium: Four Views*, Robert G. Clause, ed. Downers Grove, Illinois: InterVarsity, 1977.

Borg, M. J. *The Heart of Christianity: Rediscovering a Life of Faith*. New York: HarperCollins, 2003.

Bright, John. *The Kingdom of God*. Nashville, Tennessee: Abingdon, 1953.

Burrows, Robert J. L. "Americans Get Religion in the New Age," *Christianity Today*. Carol Stream, Illinois: Christianity Today International, May 16, 1986.

Caragounis, C. C. "Kingdom of God/Heaven," in *Dictionary of Jesus and the Gospels*, J. B. Green, S. McKnight, and I. H. Marshall, editors. Downers Grove, Illinois: InterVarsity, 1992.

Cerullo, Morris. *America in Prophecy: Sound the Alarm!* San Diego, California: Morris Cerullo World Evangelism, 2004.

Clouse, R. G. "Millennium, Views of the," in *Evangelical Dictionary of Theology*, Second Edition, W. A. Elwell, editor. Grand Rapids, Michigan: Baker Book House, 2001.

————. "Rapture of the Church," in *Evangelical Dictionary of Theology*, Second Edition, W. A. Elwell, editor. Grand Rapids, Michigan: Baker Book House, 2001.

Danker, F. W., ed. *A Greek-English Lexicon of the New Testament and Other Early Christian Literature,* 3rd ed. Chicago, Illinois: The University of Chicago Press, 2000.

Edwards, Jonathan. "Sinners in the Hands of an Angry God," in *Annals of America,* Vol. 1, 1493–1754. Chicago, Illinois: William Denton, Encyclopedia Britannica, 1968.

Evans, C. Stephen. *Existentialism: The Philosophy of Despair and the Quest for Hope.* Dallas, Texas: Probe Ministries International, 1984.

Faulkner, J. A., Murray, J., and Bromiley, G. W. "Justification," in *The International Standard Bible Encyclopedia,* Vol. 2. G. W. Bromiley, editor. Grand Rapids, Michigan: Eerdmans, 1982.

Flavel, John. *The Method of Grace: How the Holy Spirit Works.* Grand Rapids, Michigan: Baker Book House, 1977.

Ford, D. W. Cleverly. *The Ministry of the Word.* Grand Rapids, Michigan: Eerdmans, 1979.

Gaffin, R. B. *The Centrality of the Resurrection.* Grand Rapids, Michigan: Baker Book House, 1978.

———. "Kingdom of God," in *New Dictionary of Theology,* S. B. Ferguson, D. F. Wright, and J. I. Packer, editors. Downers Grove, Illinois: InterVarsity, 1988.

Gerstner, John H. *Wrongly Dividing the Word of Truth: A Critique of Dispensationalism,* Second Edition, edited by Don Kistler, Morgan. Pennsylvania: Soli Deo Gloria Publications, 2000.

Goldsworthy, G. "Kingdom of God," in *New Dictionary of Biblical Theology,* T. D. Alexander, B. S. Rosner, D. A. Carson, and G. Goldsworthy, editors. Downers Grove, Illinois: InterVarsity, 2000.

Gruenler, R. G. "Last Day, Days," in *Evangelical Dictionary of Theology,* Second Edition, W. A. Elwell, editor. Grand Rapids, Michigan: Baker Book House, 2001.

Haldeman, I. M. *Signs of the Times,* 3rd edition. New York: Charles C. Cook, 1972.

Hanegraaff, Hank. "What Is the New Age Movement". Rancho Santa Margarita, California: Christian Research Institute. [Web]: http://www.equip.org/, 2004.

Harrison, E. F. "Presence of God," in *The International Standard Bible Encyclopedia,* Vol. 3, G. W. Bromiley, editor. Grand Rapids, Michigan: Eerdmans, 1986.

Hebblethwaite, Brian. *The Christian Hope.* Grand Rapids, Michigan: Eerdmans, 1964.

Heddendorf, Russell H. "Christians in the World, but not of the World," *Presbyterian Journal,* January 1 and 8, 1986.

Heidelberg Catechism, Christian Classic Ethereal Library (CCEL) website: http://www.ccel.org/creeds/heidelberg-cat-ext.txt.

Hesselgrave, David J., and Edward Rommen. *Contextualization.* Pasadena, California: Wm. Carey Library, 2000.

Hoekema, Anthony A. *The Bible and the Future.* Grand Rapids, Michigan: Eerdmans, 1979.

Hoffecker, W. A. "Schleiermacher, Friedrich Daniel Ernst," in *Evangelical Dictionary of Theology,* Second Edition, W. A. Elwell, editor. Grand Rapids, Michigan: Baker Book House, 2001.

Holwerda, David. "The Challenge of Rudolf Bultmann," *The Reformed Journal,* November 1976.

Howard-Snyder, D. "Eschatology," in *Evangelical Dictionary of Theology,* Second Edition, W. A. Elwell, editor. Grand Rapids, Michigan: Baker Book House, 2001.

Hunt, Dave. *The Cult Explosion.* Irvine, California: Harvest House, 1980.

Hunt, Dave, and McMahon, T. A. *The Seduction of Christianity: Spiritual Discernment in the Last Days.* Eugene, Oregon: Harvest House, 1985.

Kreitzer, L. J. "Kingdom of God/Christ," in *Dictionary of Paul and His Letters,* G. F. Hawthrone, R. P. Martin, and D. G. Reid, editors. Downers Grove, Illinois: InterVarsity, 1993.

Ladd, G. E. *The Gospel of the Kingdom.* Grand Rapids, Michigan: Eerdmans, 1959.

———. "Kingdom of Christ, God, Heaven," in *Evangelical Dictionary of Theology,* Second Edition, W. A. Elwell, editor. Grand Rapids, Michigan: Baker Book House, 2001.

LaHaye, Tim. *The Beginning of the End.* Wheaton, Illinois: Tyndale, 1972.

LaHaye, Tim and Jenkins, Jerry B. *Left Behind Series,* Volumes 1–12. Carol Stream, Illinois: Tyndale House Publishers, 2004.

Lardie, Debra, et al. *Concise Dictionary of the Occult and New Age.* Grand Rapids, Michigan: Kregel Publications, 2000.

Larson, Bruce. "Hope—The Power for Your Future," *Plus,* Vol. 36, No. 10 (Part III), December 1985.

Lewis, C. S. *The Problem of Pain.* San Francisco: Harper, 2001.

Lewis, N., editor. *Roget's Thesaurus in Dictionary Form.* New York: G. P. Putnam's, Berkley edition, 1961.

Lindsey, Hal. *The Late Great Planet Earth*. New York: Bantam Books, 1976.

———. *The Terminal Generation*. New York: Bantam Books, 1977.

Lioy, Dan. *The Book of Revelation in Christological Focus*. New York: Peter Lang Publishers, 2003.

———. *The Decalogue in the Sermon on the Mount* .New York: Peter Lang Publishers, 2004.

Lithgow, John. *Footloose*. Hollywood, California: Paramount Home Video, 1984.

Louw, J. P. and Nida, E. A. eds. *Greek-English Lexicon of the New Testament: Based on Semantic Domains*, 2nd ed., vol. 1: Introduction and Domains, vol. 2: Indices. New York, New York: United Bible Societies, 1989.

Lutzer, Edwin. *How to Have a Whole Heart in a Broken World*. Wheaton, Illinois: Victor, 1987.

MacArthur, John. Sermon Tape GC 45-41, "The Security of Salvation," Part 2, 1982.

———. *Hard to Believe: The High Cost and Infinite Value of Following Jesus*. Nashville, Tennessee: Thomas Nelson Publishers, 2003.

Machen, J. Gresham. *Christianity and Liberalism*. Grand Rapids, Michigan: Eerdmans, 1923.

Martin, R. P. *The Illustrated Bible Dictionary*, Vol. 3. Wheaton, Illinois: Tyndale, 1980.

Mason, S. "Pharisees," in *Dictionary of New Testament Background*, C. A. Evans and S. E. Porter, editors. Downers Grove, Illinois: InterVarsity, 2000.

Mathison, Keith A. *Dispensationalism: Rightly Dividing the People of God?* Phillipsburg, New Jersey: P&R Publishing, 1995.

McGrath, A. E. "Justification," in *Dictionary of Paul and His Letters*, G. F. Hawthorne, R. P. Martin, and D. G. Reid, editors. Downers Grove, Illinois: InterVarsity, 1993.

Middleman, U. W. *The Market-Driven Church: The Worldly Influence of Modern Culture on the Church in America*. Wheaton, Illinois: Crossway Books, 2004.

Milne, B. A. *The Illustrated Bible Dictionary*, Vol. 2. Wheaton, Illinois: InterVarsity, 1980.

Minear, Paul S. *Christian Hope and the Second Coming*. Philadelphia, Pennsylvania: Westminster, 1954.

Moore, T. M. *Redeeming Pop Culture: A Kingdom Approach*. Phillipsburg, New Jersey: P&R Publishing, 2003.

Morris, L. "Parousia," in *The International Standard Bible Encyclopedia*, Vol. 3, G. W. Bromiley, editor. Grand Rapids, Michigan: Eerdmans, 1986.

———. "Last Days(s), Latter Days, Last Times," in *Evangelical Dictionary of Biblical Theology*, W. A. Elwell, editor. Grand Rapids, Michigan: Baker Book House, 1996.

Moule, C. F. D. *The Meaning of Hope, Biblical Series-5*. Philadelphia, Pennsylvania: Fortress, 1963.

Mouw, Richard J. *When the Kings Come Marching In*. Grand Rapids, Michigan: Eerdmans, 1983.

———. "The Waning of Hell," *The Banner*, August 24, 1987.

Noel, Ted. *I Want to Be Left Behind*. Maitland, Florida: Bible Only Press, 2002.

Ogilvie, Lloyd. *Where There's Hope, There's Life*, from the series, *Always, There Is Hope* Hollywood: Lloyd Ogilvie Ministries, Inc, 1988.

Ohlrich, Charles. *The Suffering God*. Downers Grove, Illinois: InterVarsity, 1982.

Opperwall, N. J. "Presence," in *The International Standard Bible Encyclopedia*, Vol. 3. G. W. Bromiley, editor. Grand Rapids, Michigan: Eerdmans, 1986.

Orme, A. Dan. "New Age: Religion of the Avant-Garde Middle Class," *World Magazine*. Palm Coast, Florida: World Magazine, Inc., May 5, 1986.

Osteen, Joel. *Your Best Life Now: 7 Steps to Living at Your Full Potential*. New York, New York: Warner Faith, 2004.

Packer, J. I. *Knowing God*. Downer's Grove, Illinois: InterVarsity, 1993.

———. "Justification," in *Evangelical Dictionary of Theology*, Second Edition, W. A. Elwell, editor. Grand Rapids, Michigan: Baker Book House, 2001.

Palms, Roger C. *Bible Readings on Hope*. Minneapolis, Minnesota: Augsburg, 1987.

Pierard, R. V. "Liberalism, Theological," in *Evangelical Dictionary of Theology*, Second Edition, W. A. Elwell, editor. Grand Rapids, Michigan: Baker Book House, 2001.

Plantinga Jr., Cornelius. *Engaging God's World: A Reformed Vision of Faith, Learning, and Living*. Grand Rapids, Michigan: Eerdmans, 2002.

Porter, S. E. "Holiness, Sanctification," in *Dictionary of Paul and His Letters*, G. F. Hawthorne, R. P. Martin, and D. G. Reid, editors. Downers Grove, Illinois: InterVarsity, 1993.

Poythress, Vern S. *Understanding Dispensationalists*, Second Edition. Phillipsburg, New Jersey: P&R Publishing, 1994.

Price, R. M. "Schweitzer, Albert," in *New Dictionary of Theology*, S. B. Ferguson and D. F. Wright, editors. Downers Grove, Illinois: InterVarsity, 1988.

Prior, Kenneth. *The Way of Holiness*. Downers Grove, Illinois: InterVarsity, 1982.

Roberts, Robert C. *Spirituality and Human Emotion*. Grand Rapids, Michigan: Eerdmans, 1982.

Ryken, L., Wilhoit, J. C., and Longman III, Tremper, editors. *Dictionary of Biblical Imagery*. Downers Grove, Illinois: InterVarsity Press, 1998.

Safer, Morley. "Rise of the Righteous Army," *60 Minutes*. New York: CBS Broadcasting Inc., February 8, 2004.

Schoonhoven, C. R. "Heaven," in *The International Standard Bible Encyclopedia*, Vol. 2, G. W. Bromiley, editor. Grand Rapids, Michigan: Eerdmans, 1982.

Schuller, Robert H. *Self-Esteem: The New Reformation*. Waco, Texas: Word Books, 1982.

Seesemann, H. "*peirasmos*," in *Theological Dictionary of the New Testament*, G. Kittel, ed., G.W. Bromiley, trans. Grand Rapids, Michigan: Eerdmans, 1999.

Skoglund, Elizabeth. *More Than Coping*. Minneapolis, Minnesota: World Wide, 1987.

Smedes, Lewis B. *Shame and Grace*. New York, New York: Harper Collins Publishers, 1993.

Spinks, Byran D. "Worshiping the Lamb or Entertaining the Sheep? Evaluating Evangelical Practice By the Reformed Principles of Worship," *Modern Reformation*. Philadelphia, Pennsylvania: Alliance of Confessing Evangelicals, November/December 1999.

Sproul, R. C. *The Holiness of God*. Wheaton, Illinois: Tyndale, 1985.

———. *The Last Days According to Jesus*. Grand Rapids, Michigan: Baker Book House, 1998.

Stein, R. H. 1996. "Kingdom of God," in *Evangelical Dictionary of Biblical Theology*, W. A. Elwell, editor. Grand Rapids, Michigan: Baker Book House, 1996.

Tenny, Merrill C. *New Testament Survey*. Grand Rapids, Michigan: Eerdmans, 1961.

The Net Bible. Garland, Texas: Biblical Studies Press, L.L.C., and the authors, 2001. [Web:] http://www.bible.org/netbible/index. htm.

Tolson, Jay. "The New Old-Time Religion," *U.S. News & World Report,* Washington, D.C.: U.S. News and World Report. [Web]: http://www.usnews.com/. December 8, 2003.

Vanderwaal, Cornelius. *Search the Scriptures,* vol. 10, translated by Theodore Plantinga. St. Catharines, Ontario, Canada: Paideia Press, 1979.

Van Impe, Jack. *Everything You Always Wanted to Know About Prophecy But Didn't Know Who to Ask!* Royal Oak, Michigan: Jack Van Impe Ministries, 1980.

Veith, Gene Edward. "Keeping the Faiths," *World Magazine,* Palm Coast, Florida: World Magazine, Inc., January 24, 2004.

———. "Stray Pastors," *World Magazine.* Palm Coast, Florida: World Magazine, Inc., February 7, 2004.

Vos, Gerhardus. *The Kingdom of God and the Church.* Phillipsburg, New Jersey: Presbyterian & Reformed, 1972.

Voskuil, Dennis. *Mountains into Goldmines: Robert Schuller and the Gospel of Success.* Grand Rapids, Michigan: Eerdmans, 1983.

Wells, David F. "Introduction: The Word in the World," in *The Compromised Church,* John H. Armstrong, editor. Wheaton, Illinois: Crossway Books, 1998.

Westerholm, S. "Sanctification," in *The International Standard Bible Encyclopedia,* Vol. 4, G. W. Bromiley, editor. Grand Rapids, Michigan: Eerdmans, 1988.

Whisenant, Edgar C. *On Borrowed Time.* Nashville, Tennessee: World Bible Society, 1988.

White, R. E. O. "Sanctification," in *Evangelical Dictionary of Theology,* Second Edition, W. A. Elwell, editor. Grand Rapids, Michigan: Baker Book House, 2001.

Wieand, D. J. 1982. "Hinnom, Valley of," in *The International Standard Bible Encyclopedia,* Vol. 2, G. W. Bromiley, editor. Grand Rapids, Michigan: Eerdmans, 1982.

Wiersbe, Warren. *Walking With the Giants.* Grand Rapids, Michigan: Baker Book House, 1976.

Wolterstorff, Nicholas. *Lament for a Son.* Grand Rapids, Michigan: Eerdmans, 1987.

Yarbrough, R. W. "History of Religion School," in *Evangelical Dictionary of Theology,* Second Edition, W. A. Elwell, editor. Grand Rapids, Michigan: Baker Book House, 2001.